OFFICIAL REPORT

OF THE

THIRTY - EIGHTH

INTERNATIONAL CONVENTION

OF CHRISTIAN ENDEAVOR

Held at Atlantic City,

New Jersey

July 8 - 13, 1941

First Fruits Press
Wilmore, Kentucky
c2015

First Fruits Press
The Academic Open Press of Asbury Theological Seminary
204 N. Lexington Ave., Wilmore, KY 40390
859-858-2236
first.fruits@asburyseminary.edu
asbury.to/firstfruits

LEADERS IN THE INTERNATIONAL SOCIETY

DR. DANIEL A. POLING
President

MISS PAULINE SHOEMAKER
Associate President

2

THE OFFICIAL REPORT

of the

Thirty-eighth

International Convention

of

Christian Endeavor

at

ATLANTIC CITY, NEW JERSEY

July 8-13, 1941

MR. ALVIN C. POFFENBERGER
General Chairman of the Convention Committee

Recorder

CATHERINE MILLER BALM

Editor

BERT H. DAVIS

Copyright, 1942

INTERNATIONAL SOCIETY OF CHRISTIAN ENDEAVOR
41 MT. VERNON STREET, BOSTON, MASSACHUSETTS

Printed in the United States of America

Contents

Illustrations

ATLANTIC CITY CONVENTION COMMITTEE

ALVIN C. POFFENBERGER, Chairman

Vice-chairman	Paul T. Wolcott
Vice-chairman	Reuel B. Wolford
Secretary	Miss Grace E. Tanquary
Treasurer	John H. Truex
Finance	Henry W. Leeds
Convention Bureau	A. J. Morgan
President, International Society of Christian Endeavor	Dr. Daniel A. Poling
Executive Secretary, International Society	Carroll M. Wright
President, New Jersey Union	Hugh R. McGeachie
Executive Secretary, New Jersey Union	Frederick L. Mintel
President, Atlantic County Union	Miss Florence Kappes
President, Philadelphia Union	Louis Klein, Jr.
President, Ministerial Union	Rev. W. H. B. Detwiler
Atlantic County Sunday School Association	Jacob F. Ellis
Epworth League	Robert Watson
Representative, Middle Atlantic Region, International Society	Miss Pauline Shoemaker
Representative, Middle Atlantic Region	Arch J. McQuilkin

Committee Chairmen

Banquets and Luncheons	Thomas Husselton
Decorations, Halls	A. J. Morgan
Exhibits	James C. Peacock
High School (Intermediate) Section	Mrs. W. H. B. Detwiler
Hotels	A. J. Morgan
Information	Thomas Husselton
Music	Rev. W. H. B. Detwiler
Pages and Guides	Harold V. Feyl
Parade	Carl Voelker
Park and Street Meetings	Adrian W. Phillips
Pulpit Supply	Rev. Franklin T. Buck
Radio	Norman Reed
Reception	Mrs. Raymond B. Ingersoll
Ushers	Rev. George Naylor

PROGRAM COMMITTEE

REV. J. GORDON HOWARD, D.D., Chairman

Rev. Lawrence W. Bash	Miss Pauline Shoemaker
Rev. Leslie G. Deinstadt	Rev. Arthur J. Stanley
Dr. Frank D. Getty	Dr. George Oliver Taylor
Mrs. Helen Lyon Jones	Dr. Raymond M. Veh
Norman Klauder	Reuel B. Wolford
Frederick L. Mintel	Dr. Stanley B. Vandersall, Secretary
Alvin C. Poffenberger	Dr. Daniel A. Poling, Ex-officio

DR. WM. HIRAM FOULKES
Honorary Vice President

MRS. HELEN LYON JONES
Vice President

HARRY N. HOLMES
Vice President

Vice Presidents of the International Society

DR. NORMAN V. PEALE
Vice President

REV. LAWRENCE W. BASH
Vice President

DR. J. GORDON HOWARD
Vice President

THE HONORABLE HAROLD E. STASSEN
Governor of the State of Minnesota

The awarding, for the third time, of International Youth's Distinguished Service Citation was one of the high points of interest and enthusiasm in the 38th International Christian Endeavor Convention in July. The recipient was the youngest Governor in the United States,—a man eminent in statecraft and in matters pertaining to character and religion. Those preceding him in receiving this award were: Rear Admiral Richard E. Byrd, U. S. N. Retired, in 1937, and the Honorable Herbert Clark Hoover, ex-President of the United States, in 1939. The citation is shown opposite.

International Youth's Distinguished Service

CITATION TO

Harold Edward Stassen

Harold Edward Stassen is the youngest Chief Executive in the history of the State of Minnesota and concurrently the youngest Governor in the United States. He was born April 13, 1907, is a graduate of the University of Minnesota and of the University of Minnesota Law School. He was County Attorney from 1930 until his election in 1938 to the first office of his Commonwealth.

As Chief Executive, he has simplified and reorganized the business affairs of the state, introduced wise economies and at the same time protected the essential human services - public relief, old age assistance, and general education. On the occasion of this award he is Chairman of the Governors' Conference of the United States and in personality, character and public life typifies American achievement and the spirit of American democracy at their best.

Throughout his crowded career, he has been vitally identified with the Christian church, an active member in his own communion and a dynamic leader of Christian youth. He has served as President of the Baptist Young People's Union, and is now Vice-President of the Northern Baptist Convention.

By his years and character, by his public career in government and religion, he meets the requirements of International Youth's Distinguished Service Citation and stands worthily with those who have been thus honored in the past. Among his contemporaries, Governor Stassen more than any other man typifies youth answering his country's call for sacrificial service and patriotic leadership.

Presented by the
International Society of Christian Endeavor
and the World's Christian Endeavor Union
at Atlantic City, N. J., July 8, 1941.

"The nation's youth face the future, even in these dark days, with calm courage, with a fundamental faith in Christianity, and with a determination to preserve our free way of life in America."

From Governor Stassen's Address.

The President's Greeting

Dear Dr. Poling.

The 60th Anniversary Convention of the International Society of Christian Endeavor, to which I send heartfelt greetings, meets at a time of grave crisis in the affairs of the Nation and of the world. All that we hold dearest in our national heritage is challenged.

Justice, mercy, truth and freedom are all under attack by totalitarianism which outrages the inherent dignity of human personality. Only in union shall we find strength to combat the menace which threatens free people everywhere—the tyranny of force over the lives and consciences of men.

We as people of many origins and diverse cultures and spiritual allegiances can, in full loyalty to our individual convictions, work and pray for the establishment of an international order in which the spirit of Christ shall rule. In such an order alone will our cherished freedoms, including freedom of conscience, be secure. Let us unite in labor and prayer to hasten its coming

Very sincerely yours,

(SIGNED)   *Franklin D. Roosevelt*

July 4, 1941.

I

As the Clouds Rose

THAT dismal drizzle stopped. The sun stabbed through the scattering clouds. Many days of rain were ending along the eastern seacoast.

As sunlight glistened again on the tossing ocean and on the golden sands at Atlantic City, it was as if lights went on and a curtain rose on the Sixtieth Anniversary International Christian Endeavor Convention.

And this was the *Rainbow* Jubilee indeed! The Convention arrived in sunlight, while the last traces of rain and fog scudded away. Again "the capital city of North American hospitality," as Dr. Manson Doyle of Canada was to name it, wore its gayest smiles to greet the delegates.

Preview of a Convention

By noon of Tuesday, July 8, thousands of delegates had registered at Convention Hall and were eagerly viewing beach and Boardwalk. Very early arrivals had time now for a swim, and even the delegates from California admired the excellence of this bathing beach! Delegates came by train and automobile; two dozen Tennessee Endeavorers drove day and night through unceasing rain. Donald Lane of Holland, Michigan, had hitchhiked from mid-continent to attend these meetings. Margaret Ballachey came from Trinidad, British West Indies, bringing the greetings of the Union of Young People's Christian Associations there.

A little group gloated at having attended another Atlantic City Convention—held thirty years before. Here was Clara Dohme of Baltimore, showing the badges from Conventions attended all the years since 1894. She has missed only three International Conventions and more than made up for the omissions by attending seven of the eleven World's Conventions of Christian Endeavor. Here was Dr. Samuel W. Steckel of Atlantic City, whose first Convention was New York, 1892, and who vividly remembers the World's Convention in London in 1900. Here was the Rev. Robert Elwood, chosen to write notes of the 1941 gathering for the Atlantic City newspapers, and so repeating an assignment that had come to him in far-away 1911.

"A great Convention,—Atlantic City 1911!" these veterans declared. "Dr. Clark was here, of course, and William Shaw, the dynamic General Secretary of Christian Endeavor."

CARROLL M. WRIGHT
Executive Sec'y and Treasurer

STANLEY B. VANDERSALL
Associate Secretary

ERNEST S. MARKS
Field Secretary

WILLIAM J. VON MINDEN
Auditor

Staff Officers of the International Society

President Taft came to the Convention banquet, and gave a stirring address before the Convention.

That Convention held before the nation a challenge, "A Saloonless Nation by 1920," and the nation made that challenge into fact!

There was a young state Field Secretary—from Ohio, wasn't he?— who was very active in the 1911 Convention. A promising young man— that Dan Poling. The "promising young man" in 1941 launched the program by presiding at a meeting of the Board of Trustees of the International Society of Christian Endeavor in the Hotel Dennis. For sixteen years Dr. Daniel A. Poling had been President of the International Society of Christian Endeavor, and President of the World's Christian Endeavor Union since Dr. Clark's death in 1927.

While delegates registered and viewed the state exhibits and the literature exhibits, and went swimming, and rushed back and forth along the Boardwalk in laughing groups, the trustees finished a two-day session filled with thoughtful consideration of Christian Endeavor's policies and program. The nominating committee ended its deliberations and was ready to present its slate of officers to the Board of Trustees.

Morning—noon—and now afternoon.

At 4:30 the inimitable Homer Rodeheaver appeared in the Assembly Hall, bearing his faithful trombone, and was instantly surrounded by a host of delegates eager to be in the Convention chorus. For the first time in Christian Endeavor history, the chorus was to be made up of experienced choir singers drawn from the delegations. At previous Conventions local singers have composed the chorus, and rehearsed for weeks preceding the first mass meeting. Be it said at once that *this* chorus, which rehearsed only for brief periods during the Convention's free time, was outstandingly good! Charming and talented Gertrude Kirsteen of Atlantic City was the Convention organist and contributed much to the beauty of the musical program.

A Prayer Service Begins the Program

In an upper room looking out over the ocean—calm and peaceful now that the storm had ended—delegates met for the pre-Convention service of prayer. Dr. J. Arthur Heck of the Evangelical Church presided at this session, which began with the singing of "Living for Jesus." In place of a Scripture reading twenty-two Endeavorers repeated their favorite Bible passages. Well-loved choruses from other Conventions were sung—"He Lives!" "Into My Heart," "Let the Beauty of Jesus Be Seen in Me." Dr. Heck's brief informal talk was based on the thought (Rom. 8:9), "If any man have not the spirit of Christ, he is none of his," and suggested that the hearts of all be attuned to the truth and opened to the leading of the Holy Spirit. He urged the young people to exercise the spirit of Christ in all relationships, in thinking and in conduct, and by their lives to draw others to Christ. Quietly the delegates listened to this talk. Earnestly they prayed for God's blessing on the Convention.

And Now, the First Big Meeting of All Delegates

Morning—afternoon—finally night.

As the many lights of Atlantic City began to twinkle and glow, the delegates looked out to sea. On this shore, all the sparkle and gaiety of lovely Atlantic City; on the shore beyond the sea, darkness and terror and war. *What could the Thirty-eighth International Christian Endeavor Convention mean at such a time as this? What could Christian young people do to help a world in turmoil?*

Thoughtfully, six thousand young people went into the Convention Hall.

II

The Rainbow Jubilee Convention Begins

CONVENTIONS are an old story to Atlantic City's Convention Auditorium. Its beautiful Assembly Hall, with windows wide to the sea breezes, ceiling bright with the signs of the Zodiac, dignified blue-curtained stage now decorated only with lacy ferns and snowy gladioli, has been the setting for many memorable gatherings.

And Conventions are an old story to Christian Endeavor!

Yet there was an unusual thrill for those who entered Assembly Hall for the first session of the Thirty-eighth International Christian Endeavor Convention. Unmistakably, an event of exceptional significance was about to begin. The very air tingled.

Anticipation shone in the faces of the great host of young people, singing and cheering in their state delegations. Their lips sang tuneful state songs, but their eyes were upon the great stage. They watched eagerly for the entrance of Dr. Poling.

Thunderous applause greeted the appearance of the well-loved President of the International Society of Christian Endeavor and Mrs. Poling. They were followed by the other officers of the International Society and Song Leader Homer Rodeheaver, who drew a special round of applause. Mr. Rodeheaver led the Convention in a brief service of song. The chorus, in a great stand rising from the floor on the right-front corner of the Assembly Hall, sang as if its members had made music together for years.

Then—an expectant hush—and the signal came to announce that from this time the Convention program was being broadcast to the nation.

Now the Nation Listens In

Doris Doe, charming and golden-voiced contralto of the Metropolitan Opera Company, sang "Alleluia," by Humel, assisted by the Convention chorus.

Then the Convention rose and listened in respectful silence to the message read by Vice-president Harry N. Holmes,—the message of Franklin D. Roosevelt, President of the United States of America, giving his heartfelt greetings to the Convention just beginning, and closing with the appropriate words:

We as a people of many origins and diverse cultures and spiritual allegiances can, in full loyalty to our individual convictions, work and pray for the establishment of an international order in which the spirit of Christ shall rule. In such an order alone will our cherished freedoms, including freedom of conscience, be secure. Let us unite in labor and in prayer to hasten its coming.

The President's message is reproduced in full on another page of this Report.

While these opening moments set the pleasant but purposeful spirit of the still young Convention, a clear-eyed, firm-chinned young man was to be seen sitting beside President Poling on the platform.

Minnesota delegates almost burst with pride to see him sitting there. In more than one sense he was one of them—in recent years a leader among them in Christian youth activities and now the guest of honor of the International Christian Endeavor Convention.

For the youngest Governor was here, a man whose achievements could well be the pride of men carrying a far heavier weight of years.

Christian Endeavor Honors a Governor

But let Dr. Poling, presenting International Youth's Distinguished Service Citation to the Governor of Minnesota, tell what manner of man has come to the Atlantic City Convention, to address the young people and their nation listening in.

Said the Christian Endeavor President:

Harold Edward Stassen is the youngest Chief Executive in the history of the state of Minnesota and concurrently the youngest Governor in the United States. He was born April 13, 1907; is a graduate of the University of Minnesota and of the University of Minnesota Law School. He was County Attorney from 1930 until his election in 1938 to the first office of his Commonwealth.

As Chief Executive, he has simplified and reorganized the business affairs of the state, introduced wise economies, and at the same time protected the essential human services—public relief, old age assistance, and general education. On the occasion of this award he is Chairman of the Governors' Conference of the United States, and in personality, character and public life typifies American achievement and the spirit of American democracy at their best.

Throughout his crowded career, he has been vitally identified with the Christian Church, an active member in his own communion and a dynamic leader of Christian youth. He has served as President of the Baptist Young People's Union, and is now Vice-president of the Northern Baptist Convention.

By his years and character, by his public career in government and religion, he meets the requirements of International Youth's Distinguished Service Citation and stands worthily with those who have been thus honored in the past. Among his contemporaries, Governor Stassen more than any other man typifies youth answering his country's call for sacrificial service and leadership.

Later Gordon E. Pearson, President of the Minnesota Christian Endeavor Union, was to say of the 1941 recipient of an award earlier presented to Rear Admiral Richard E. Byrd and the Hon. Herbert Hoover, former President of the United States:

"The Endeavorers of Minnesota know and appreciate the sterling character of our beloved Governor and we are happy for the honor which has been bestowed on him."

Accepting the Award and thanking the Convention and Dr. Poling for this tribute, Minnesota's Governor called on Christian youth to take its place in meeting the problems of the present age. The address follows:

Governor Stassen Receives the Citation
from President Poling

Address of Acceptance by

GOVERNOR HAROLD E. STASSEN

I accept this unusual honor conferred by the World's Christian Endeavor Union, but I trust I may be permitted to accept it not so much in a personal sense, but rather as a representative of a great throng of young men and young women of this nation, even as those gathered here in this Convention Hall, who believe in the principles of Christianity, who hold fast to the concepts of democracy, and who seek to interpret both into action to meet the problems of the day.

I should like to accept this citation in this manner, as a representative of this movement of youth, because the accomplishments in our State of Minnesota, which appear to have largely given rise to this honor, have not been an individual accomplishment so much as they have been the result of unusual and widespread cooperation and coordination of a great number of my fellow citizens, with our young people in the front rank, striving toward objectives and ideals inherent in both our religious concepts and our form of government.

Furthermore, our success in this nation in meeting the challenge of the days ahead will be largely measured by the degree in which large numbers of our young people work together in the intelligent translation of our ideals into determined and courageous action.

Youth Faces Realities and Principles

This generation, for which I speak, is the youth who have reached their years of maturity during the last decade and more of economic depression. They have experienced the heartaches and disappointments of days and months, and even years, of vainly seeking a place in the productive stream of commerce. They are the generation that is now being called upon to man the armed forces of this country to strengthen the defenses of this nation on land, at sea, and in the air. They are also being enrolled in large numbers as youthful and comparatively unskilled workmen to expand the production of the mechanical means of national defense. With these experiences they have been giving more than ordinary thought and consideration to fundamental concepts and basic principles of life and of action.

On their behalf I say tonight, *they face the future, even in these dark days, with calm courage, with a fundamental faith in Christianity, and with a determination to preserve our free way of life in America.*

As we see it, the greatest need before us is to interpret the principles of our religion and of our democracy into action in meeting the social, economic, political and international problems of the days ahead. We must strengthen our churches, we must increase the number of our children and of our youth securing Christian training and education.

We commend the significant contribution to Christian education and the church made by the World's Christian Endeavor Union with its four millions under the inspiring leadership of your President, Dr. Poling.

We must increase the understanding of the methods of democracy, but we must go beyond, and with frankness and with ingenuity develop ways of applying these concepts to the new problems that arise in a world that does not stand still.

We recognize that the greatness of this nation is due not only to the great courage at Valley Forge and the victories against odds by the Thirteen Colonies, but also to the vision, the statesmanship and the ingenious creation of new mechanics of government at the Constitutional Convention.

Standing for the Right

One of the greatest moments in our history came during that Constitutional Convention when, after long hours of discussion and divergence of views and seeming impossibility of securing a constructive result, George Washington rose and said:—"If to please the people we adopt that of which we ourselves do not approve, how can we afterwards defend our work? Let us raise a standard to which the wise and honest can repair; the event is in the hands of God." This great utterance brought to that Constitutional Convention its turning point, and with courage the delegates drafted the Constitution of these United States, striking out in a pioneering way to a new governmental structure. You know what happened. . . . The people rallied to its support; it was adopted and became the foundation for this great, free country.

We recognize further that just a generation ago the soldiers of our country fought in a World War. They fought with the same courage and the same success as did our founding fathers, but when the peace came there was a failure to develop the means by which that peace could be translated into the foundation for justice and a continuing peace between the nations of the world. Thus, we now have once again the horrors of war with millions of people suffering untold hardships and misery and death, as the brutal attempt is made to substitute the rule of force for the laws of justice.

Facing realistically the tragedy of this war, we know that it has had, and will have, a tremendous effect upon the future of the men and women and children of this nation and of every other nation in the world. We cannot ignore these facts—we must face them. Neither realistically, nor in keeping with our basic principles, can we wrap the cloak of our rich resources around us, lift our chins, look neither to the East or West, and go lightly on our way.

The World Is a Neighborhood

With the great changes in communication and transportation, what happens in one part of the world very quickly and directly affects the people in other parts of the world. The great challenge to the generation ahead is not only to restore the rule of justice and prevent the supremacy of brutal force and duplicity, but also to work out the means and the machinery for the functioning of a system of justice between the peoples of all nations in keeping with our fundamental principles of the rights of each individual human being and in keeping with the injunction of Him who said—"Go ye into all nations."

In meeting this crisis we see it as our task to aid in maintaining support and respect for and confidence in our duly selected leaders of the government and of the Armed Forces, to increase tolerance and understanding between our people and prevent bitterness and hatred from arising, to shun narrow nationalism and petty partisanship, to protect minorities and support majorities, to stand back of those who are called into service, to seek out every means of building up the strength of our nation in its devotion to the cause of freedom and justice.

Called into Partnership

In this same spirit we must work out the means of improving the relationship between groups of our people within the nation. The relationship between labor and management must be improved. They must be looked upon as partners and not as antagonists. The employer cannot with immunity exploit labor, and neither can labor with immunity injure the employer. A basic recognition of each other's rights and problems must, around a conference table to an increasing degree, take the place of strikes, lockouts and violence.

We must to an increasing degree develop the means of meeting the needs of those of our people who are handicapped and dependent, while at the same time maintaining their morale and their courage. We must maintain the financial soundness of our governmental structure and add to the confidence of the people in its integrity and its efficiency. There must be a never ending advance on all fronts of the new problems that ever arise.

This generation, for which I speak tonight, recognizes this challenge and is rising to meet it, trained and strengthened by their own experiences in the years that have gone by. They are holding fast to fundamentals and yet, with a pioneering spirit, forging ahead. They are determined that this country shall meet its responsibility as a great Christian nation and that its ideals shall live through definite courageous steps contributing to the future welfare of the men and women and little children, not only within its borders, but in all other parts of the world. Christianity is the only solution of the world's problems.

With the conclusion of Governor Stassen's address the radio broadcast ended. And then Dr. Poling turned to the Governor and said:

"Now that we are alone we wish to endorse all that you have said, sir. We shall follow you in your own career with our prayers and nominate you for President of the United States. We count you one of us! God bless you and give you increasing success."

Atlantic City Welcomes the Delegates

Because of the timing of the broadcast, the usual order of a Convention session had been somewhat altered. The worship service, "We Praise Thee, O God," led by Miss Genevieve McCulloch, President of the Iowa Christian Endeavor Union, followed Governor Stassen's address. Then came the official expression of Atlantic City's welcome to the delegates, already well assured.

Genial Mayor Thomas G. Taggart, Jr., came personally to welcome the delegates and to present the key of the city to Dr. Poling. Mayor Taggart expressed pride that Atlantic City had been chosen for the Rainbow Jubilee Convention, described some of the attractions it offered to the delegates, and wished for every delegate a happy and inspiring time.

Alvin C. Poffenberger, prominent in religious, civic and business affairs in Atlantic City, and General Chairman of the Convention Committee, said in welcoming the Convention:

The Eighth Annual Children's Week in Atlantic City has just closed. This is the week when all children under twelve years of age, if accompanied by adult members of their family, are entertained complimentarily by many of the hotels of Atlantic City. What a happy experience it has been to have a part in the program arranged for the children, some 2500, the future America!

And now, immediately following, we welcome to our shores the older youth of America, some five thousand strong, with their leaders. Our facilities are yours to enjoy. May the dust-free air, sunshine and ever-changing sea be a real inspiration to you during your sojourn here.

As Dr. A. J. Stoddard, Superintendent of Schools of Philadelphia, in an address delivered before the graduating class of the Atlantic City schools this year, said: "We are now tremendously concerned with the problem of winning democracy. Our forefathers did not give us freedom—but a better chance to win it. Freedom is a method of accomplishment." And looking at the young men and women with earnestness, Dr. Stoddard said: "It is up to you. The future of our country depends upon you." May I reiterate those words of Dr. Stoddard? It is a challenge to the Christian young men and women of America. I know you will meet that challenge.

And now, Dr. Poling, I wish to present to you a photograph taken during the Convention of the International Christian Endeavor held in Atlantic City in July, 1911, just thirty years ago. It is a picture of dinner guests of Cap'n John L. Young, pioneer amusement man of Atlantic City, who owned and operated the Million Dollar Pier for years. His residence was on the Pier—No. 1 Atlantic Ocean. Among the guests seated at that dinner were President William Howard Taft, Russell H. Conwell, famed for his glorious "Acres of Diamonds" sermon, Evangeline Booth, Booker T. Washington.

Also, I wish to present to you, Dr. Poling, a gavel and block, both of which were made from wood secured from Cap'n John L. Young's home—No. 1 Atlantic Ocean, where thirty years ago the dinner was held honoring William Howard Taft, the President of the United States, and outstanding leaders in Christian Endeavor.

Dr. Poling, in accepting these gifts, smilingly declared, "Now that I have this gavel, I declare the Thirty-eighth International Christian Endeavor Convention in session." The delegates laughed and cheered; the Convention had been too significantly in session for anyone to have missed the traditional opening sentence!

Referring to the 1911 Convention, Dr. Poling said, "I attended that convention as a stripling youth from Ohio. I did not rate an invitation to that dinner at which this photograph was taken."

He then paid tribute to Dr. William Shaw, "Grand Marshal of Christian Endeavor" in 1911, who gave fifty-eight of his years in Christian Endeavor's service. Now eighty-one years old and living quietly in California, he sent cordial greetings to the 1941 Convention. This greeting and a cablegram from Dr. James Kelly of Scotland were read by Dr. Poling.

Dr. W. A. MacTaggart, Christian Endeavor leader of Canada and equally beloved in the United States, graciously replied to the speeches of welcome to Atlantic City. Referring to the place of Christian Endeavor in this time of crisis, Dr. MacTaggart said, "We shall march on when *the others* have ceased to march!"

Special guests who were introduced by Dr. Poling were Dr. Robert Ellwood, veteran of the 1911 Convention, and Dr. Adolph Keller of Europe, famous religious leader and talented musician. It was Dr. Keller who played the organ when Kaiser Wilhelm II attended the dedication of the German Church in Jerusalem years ago.

There were no more dramatic moments in the whole Convention than those when the delegates listened, spell-bound, to Doris Doe's singing of "Land of Hope and Glory" at the opening session. Many eyes were tear-dimmed and in many hearts were prayers for fellow Endeavorers now fighting for freedom for all mankind.

After the offering, Mr. Rodeheaver presented Mrs. Poling to the Convention. Said she, "May I express to you the wish that these trying years may be most fruitful for you in leadership of your young people in the cause of Jesus."

Outstanding Leaders Introduced

It is always interesting to meet the active men and women who are the present-day leaders of Christian Endeavor in the vast continent of North America. Delegates were glad, then, to have Dr. Stanley B. Vandersall present the leaders of denominational young people's work and Carroll M. Wright present the regional officers and departmental superintendents of the International Society of Christian Endeavor and the Field Secretaries of the State Unions. Most of the men and women presented would be met daily in the educational conferences, when they would be helpful and inspiring teachers.

Said Dr. Vandersall in presenting the denominational young people's leaders:

The ties of Christian Endeavor are many. There are ties to the homes from which boys and girls come to Junior Christian Endeavor societies, and from which their older brothers and sisters come to the High School and Young People's societies.

There are ties to the schools where children and youth receive culture for their minds and the establishment of ideals for their lives.

There are ties to the churches where most Christian Endeavor societies have their homes.

There are ties to the Sunday schools and missionary agencies, ties to colleges and seminaries, ties to high schools, to temperance and citizenship agencies—all of them great and good.

But we think tonight of ties and connections which are vital to the life and work of the International Society of Christian Endeavor. Through all its sixty years Christian Endeavor has belonged to the churches. Its stalwart supporters have always been men and women in the pulpit and in other places of leadership in the supporting denominations.

No group of such supporters is deserving of more recognition than that group of men and women which bears the title of "leaders of young people's work in the denominations." Some of them are editors, some are general secretaries, some are teachers— all are travelers and leaders.

They are all valued trustees of the International Society, but they are more than that. They are strong in counsel, strong in friendship, strong in labors—true comrades in the cause of and for youth, youth in connection with Christ and youth in connection with the church.

It is my personal pleasure to state that I call these men and women my friends, and as I present them to the Convention I do so with pride and with an open expression of appreciation for all that they mean to the cause of Christian Endeavor. Dr. Poling, I take pleasure in presenting, one at a time, these strong leaders of young people in the denominations of Christian Endeavor.

Denominational leaders presented were:

Dr. Manson Doyle, United Church of Canada
Dr. Frank D. Getty, Presbyterian Church, U. S. A.
Martin Harvey, A.M.E. Zion Church
Dr. J. Arthur Heck, Evangelical Church
Richard Hoiland, American Baptist Publication Society
Dr. J. Gordon Howard, United Brethren in Christ
Dr. S. S. Morris, A. M. E. Church

MISS DORIS DOE
Metropolitan Opera Contralto

DR. RAYMOND M. VEH
Director, High School Division of the
Convention

DR. J. GORDON HOWARD
Chairman of the Program Committee

HOMER RODEHEAVER
Convention Song Director

Rev. Roy Schreiner, Churches of God
Moses M. Shaw, United Presbyterian Church
Dr. George Oliver Taylor, Disciples of Christ
Dr. Robert W. Gammon, Congregational-Christian Church
Dr. Raymond M. Veh, Editor, The Evangelical Crusader
Rev. Herbert L. Minard, Editor, The Front Rank

Mr. Wright, with a gracious word of appreciation for their faithful service, presented the following:

VICE-PRESIDENTS IN CHARGE OF REGIONS

Kenneth W. Swain, North Atlantic Region
Reuel B. Wolford, Middle Atlantic Region
Miss Sarah E. McCullagh, Great Lakes Region
Albert Arend, Pacific Region

DEPARTMENTAL SUPERINTENDENTS

Mrs. Catherine M. Balm, Social and Recreational Department
Ernest R. Bryan, World Peace Department
Miss Geneva Craig, Devotional (Prayer Meeting) Department
Mrs. L. C. Greene, High School (Intermediate) Department
Mrs. Reba Rickman, Extension and Lookout Department

FIELD SECRETARIES OF STATE UNIONS

Howard J. Duven, Iowa
Warren G. Hoopes, Pennsylvania
Miss Dorothy Lehman, Indiana
Ernest S. Marks, Michigan
Frederick L. Mintel, New Jersey
Rev. Ellis R. Shaw, California
P. Marion Simms, Jr., New Mexico
Rev. James A. Thomas, Ohio
Rev. George H. Wilson, Illinois

A Message from Mother Clark

Three times during the Convention messages from Mrs. Francis E. Clark, wife of the founder of Christian Endeavor, and his faithful co-worker, were received with joy by the Convention. "Mother" Clark, now over ninety years of age, lives quietly in New England and sent this message for the first session of the Convention:

Dear Christian Endeavor Friends in the Convention at Atlantic City:

I am glad to send you my greetings and best wishes on this our sixtieth anniversary when so many thousands of Endeavorers are gathered in the great Convention. I know that we all are looking back with gratitude over the years that have been filled with the Lord's blessing on the work we have tried to do for Him. Looking forward, also, with courage to the years that are before us, trusting in the Lord Jesus Christ for strength as we strive to do more earnest and faithful service for Christ and the Church.

May every one of us be glad to be a member of the great host of Endeavorers, all seeking to do, each day, what our Master would like to have us do. As individuals, we may not feel that we count for much, but together we can be sure that our service will help to make this world a better place to live in.

Shall we not, each one of us, pray this prayer every morning as we begin our day, "Lord, give us strength, we pray, to live our life this day. To live it right, with all our might, without mistake, as for Thy sake."

Wishing for you and the Convention every blessing from our Lord, I am your friend, Harriet A. Clark.

Following the reading of this message, the Convention arose to express in prayer youth's gratitude for the life of Mother Clark.

Then Miss Doe sang, while the young people hummed, "Softly and Tenderly Jesus Is Calling."

Governor Stassen Reaches a High Point

"Always—For Christ and the Church" -- Presidential Night

L ONG before the time for the service of praise on Wednesday night, every seat in the vast Assembly Hall was filled. Not only was every delegate present, but in addition hundreds of members of the Baptist Temple in Philadelphia, of which Dr. Poling is pastor, had come to honor him on this Presidential Night. Harry N. Holmes, Vice-president of the International Society of Christian Endeavor, presided in his genial, gracious manner. Mr. Rodeheaver excelled in leading the singing; the Convention sang as one mighty, jubilant voice.

A worship service of exceptional interest was conducted by Dr. J. Gordon Howard, Chairman of the Convention Program Committee. A beautifully colored motion-picture film, "Hills and the Sea," was shown, with Scripture verses appropriate to the scenes of wonder and beauty.

An anthem by the Convention chorus and a generous offering concluded the first part of the session.

Then, with eloquence true to the best tradition of Christian Endeavor leadership, Associate President Lawrence W. Bash, of Auburn, Nebraska, addressed the Convention.

Address of the Associate President,
REV. LAWRENCE W. BASH

God is shaking the world today, and everything that isn't fast is coming loose!

Inherited loyalties to institutions and causes which served their day but have lost their sense of mission are collapsing about us. In this cataclysm there can survive only those institutions and movements which are firmly grounded on unshakeable foundations. In the midst of ruin there will remain only that which serves the vital needs of men. Only that will persist through which the inscrutable Purpose of God may bless men.

The contrast between that which draws its life from the eternal verities of God and that which withers upon the precarious resources and ingenuities of men is well-drawn in the First Psalm. "He shall be like a tree planted by the rivers of water. His leaf also shall not wither, and whatsoever he doeth shall prosper. The ungodly are not so, but are like the chaff which the wind driveth away. . The Lord knoweth the way of the righteous, but the way of the ungodly shall perish."

The chaff is being separated from the wheat today. In this time of wanton destruction and chaotic confusion, we see the hand of God, for it is He who "turnest man to destruction." There was no other way than that the world should suffer for its sins, for "He will by no means clear the guilty."

God's Way Shall Remain

Yet as surely as that which violates the purpose of God must perish, so surely shall that remain which belongs to God. "Of his kingdom there shall be no end." We take strength and courage in the admonition, "Be ye therefore steadfast, unmoveable, always abounding in the work of the Lord, forasmuch as ye know that your labor *is not in vain* in the Lord."

And still, our faith in the imperishability of truth is confronted with the sober fact that the world has been filled with institutions which were created with good purpose, yet perished. Churches *have* died. A thousand letter-head committees, all established with good intentions for the uplift and enlightenment of humanity, are here today, forgotten tomorrow. Good intentions do not insure immortality to any institution. Only the strong and the fit can survive.

What does the future hold for Christian Endeavor? In the shaking of the world and of all human endeavors, will Christian Endeavor stand fast? I believe it will! I believe it will endure because it is strong with the strength of truth.

Remember This Triangle of Faith

The triangle is said to be the strongest geometrical form. I give you a triangle of strength, a trinity of faith in Christian Endeavor. It is a faith illumined by sixty glorious years, a faith dynamic in its promise of the years to come.

The base of the triangle rests upon God the Father, Creator, and Sustainer. Only that shall endure which is of Him. Does Christian Endeavor find its place in the purpose of God? The past reveals the future, for He is "the same yesterday, today, and forever." I believe Christian Endeavor is strong in its foundation because of the rich blessings God has poured out upon and through the movement. "He that abideth in me, and I in him, the same bringeth forth much fruit; for without me ye can do nothing."

Christian Endeavor has been blessed in its leadership. For more than forty years the blessed, saintly Francis E. Clark gave his life in the calling of youth to the standard of Christ. And when the mantle of leadership fell from his shoulders, it passed to America's dynamic statesman for Christ, Daniel A. Poling. How these men have moved their generations!

And there is a special place in all our hearts for that dear little lady, Christian Endeavor's most precious treasure, Mother Clark! How richly, too, has our movement been blessed in the "legion of the inconspicuous" who have served in their own quiet places of responsibility, unheralded, perhaps unthanked, but faithful through the years.

Christian Endeavor has been blessed in its fruits. It has poured a stream of consecrated leadership into the church. There are hosts of Christian Endeavorers in the mission field. How many ministers found their call through Christian Endeavor? (Not to mention those who found a wife in Christian Endeavor!) The church has been aroused to the needs and potentialities of youth. Youth has been awakened to spiritual realities.

As God has led Christian Endeavor through these sixty years, so may He lead her in days to come. Upon that conviction, as a firm foundation, we rest our trinity of faith.

A Movement Close to Life

Some auspicious programs fail because they do not come to grips with the realities of human nature. Christian Endeavor is close to life. It was not launched as an impressive national organization, but it was a growth, almost unbelievably rapid, because it met the needs of youth.

The spirit of Christian Endeavor is one which appeals to the best in youth. It cannot be caught in the cramped confines of wordy definitions. But it cannot be missed in Christian Endeavor gatherings. Wherever you go, from Maine to California, you will find Christian Endeavor meetings different from just any youth meetings. To call the spirit evangelistic is to hint at its nature. One text always fitting in a Christian Endeavor meeting is the Good Confession of Faith, "Thou art the Christ, the son of the living God."

The spirit of Christian Endeavor has at its heart the conviction that man's most fundamental need is a right relationship with God.

The Recognition of Christ

A program which builds upon any other assumption is bound to end in futility. As one prominent minister puts it, "Not only do we need to get people out of the slums, we need also to get the slums out of people." The first principle of Christian Endeavor is confession of Christ.

In these days when we casually and easily talk of a nation's or an institution's mission to save the world, we must not forget that the primary task is the saving and redeeming of *men*. None of our bright, new worlds will endure unless they are composed of men who have found life in Christ.

Without this spirit of personal accountability to Christ, the most pretentious movement man can launch would be but sounding brass and tinkling cymbal. God could not bless it, for He would not be in it.

Christian Endeavor starts here: "Trusting in the Lord Jesus Christ for strength, I promise Him that I will strive to do whatever He would have me do." This is a full committal to Christ and His way of life. And youth responds!

Move On, Youth!

But it is not sufficient that we have this primary basic attitude. We must move on from it into life. As some writer suggests: "No house can stand without a foundation. But who wants to live in a foundation?"

And so Christian Endeavor presents a program for Christian living, training, and action. The program furnishes channels through which the spirit flows into every area of life. Christian Endeavor need not apologize for its program. It begins with individual disciplines—with commitment to Christ, with an ever-deepening spiritual life through Bible study, prayer, worship experiences, stewardship, and training in the disciplines of the spiritual life. It reaches into the church with a vital program of church activities, emphasis on church attendance and support, the training of leadership for the church, the study of God's Book week after week and the developing of loyalty to the local and world-wide church.

It opens doors of opportunity to put the principles of Christ into effective operation in the local community and the nation, through its comprehensive interdenominational fellowship. Consider the witness of Christian Endeavor in the fields of beverage alcohol, narcotics, unworthy advertising, gambling, the prostitution of the Lord's Day, and race relationships, to mention but a few.

And the scope and influence of Christian Endeavor are not provincial or national. Through its world-wide outreach, its testimony for peace and good will among nations transcends all national boundaries and limitations. How well it does this is suggested by the host of missionaries who found their inspiration through Christian Endeavor.

Here, then, is a program! Here, then, is a vital, creative spirit! And youth responds, for this meets the needs of youth—a yearning for the challenge of great inspiration, a longing for direction into paths of useful service. Christian Endeavor is strong because it meets the needs of youth!

Loyalty's Place in Life

The final side of the triangle, the third element of this trinity, is the loyalty of individual Christian Endeavorers. Now a movement may be theologically correct; it may set up on paper a splendid program. But it moves not at all until that spirit and that program catch fire in the hearts of people. Those worthy institutions which have passed out of existence during the history of mankind have usually failed at this point. Hearts grew cold. The disappearance of many rural churches will illustrate. Thousands have closed in the past three decades. Why? With new means of transportation and communication, the interests of their constituencies have come to center in the towns. The people's loyalty has lessened; they have been weaned away. Where this loyalty continues unabated, the church flourishes. When hearts grow cold it dies. Even the Church of God waits upon the burning hearts of men.

What of the strength of Christian Endeavor here? A moment's observation will hearten us. Through the years of depression we have come, with budgets trimmed, smaller staffs, financial problems. Yet from coast to coast we find youth rallying to Christian Endeavor. This is not wishful thinking. For one example, there is greater demand on publishing houses for Christian Endeavor materials than there has been in a decade. This is a matter of statistical fact.

You and I have seen Christian youth giving itself without stint in the leadership of Christian Endeavor. We have seen boys and girls of high school years who took the time to lead effectively in the local societies. We have seen the titanic labors of those who serve in the larger way—in union responsibilities. We know of the sacrificial giving of money, of time, and of ability that the message of Christian Endeavor might be heard. We know that of there has never been a youth movement which has so effectually challenged youth to give of its best for the Master.

Let Us Now Make History

But our concern is not so much with the reading of past history, no matter how pleasant, as it is with the writing of future history. What of the future? Is the loyalty of those of us of this present generation as strong? Will the steadfast devotion of our hearts complete this triangle of strength to assure the future?

We stand in Atlantic City in a significant place. Backward, we trace the story of Christian Endeavor through sixty years, and there is glory written over it. Forward, we face this embattled world, with change and decay, destruction and despair on every hand. What message has Christian Endeavor today? *"Always—For Christ and the Church!"*

May that challenge tingle in our veins as it did for the generations that marched before us! May it kindle the fires of a holy enthusiasm within our hearts. May it draw from us the staunch loyalty that they gave. The trinity of faith in Christian Endeavor—the blessing of God, meeting the needs of youth, the allegiance of those who believe themselves to be "fellow-workers with God." In this trinity is strength, strength to endure, to serve, to bless.

God is shaking the world—but there are some things that are unshakeable!

President Poling Is Introduced

And now, called anew to thoughtfulness and reconsecration by the stirring and eloquent message of the slim young Associate President, the audience in Assembly Hall was to hear the biennial message of Dr. Poling.

This climactic address introduced a novel feature, long to be remembered.

The reports of Christian Endeavor progress in many lands which came toward the close of the World's Union President's address were given in brief dramatic paragraphs by young men and young women wearing the native costumes of twenty-one countries.

With the Assembly Hall lighting dimmed, a shaft of brilliance picked out first one and then another of these young people where they stood.

But now we are listening to Harry N. Holmes, Vice-President of the International Society, as he presents Christian Endeavor's chief.

"When we think of courage we think of Daniel of the Old Testament," are Mr. Holmes' words.

"When we think of the love of the woods and the open spaces, we think of Daniel Boone.

"When we think of eloquence, we think of Daniel Webster.

"I present to you one who combines the qualities of them all—the President of the World's Christian Endeavor Union, our Daniel A. Poling!"

The complete text of Dr. Poling's Presidential Address follows in the next chapter. First, however, let us consider the impact of that address on the Convention and on the nation and in far-flung countries of the world.

Those who could not be present to catch the spirit of the address on the night of its delivery were to be reminded on the following Sunday afternoon by Dr. Walter W. Van Kirk in a nation-wide N. B. C. broadcast that an event of outstanding importance had occurred in the crowded Assembly Hall this July night.

Devoting his entire period of the immensely popular broadcast feature, "Religion in the News," to this youth Convention and its Presidential Address and the coming two-year program, Dr. Van Kirk said:

It was Dr. Poling who set the tempo of the Convention and provided the leadership around which Christian Endeavor will rally its forces in the quest for a warless world. He wasn't satisfied with words. Not Dan Poling! He presented a seven-point program designed to achieve peace in our time

And here's the program:

1—*America's support of a world agency for the administration of world affairs,—this without interference with purely internal affairs.*

2—*America's support of police power for such an administration of world affairs.*

3—*America's support of open economic frontiers, with free access to raw materials and natural resources, and with reciprocal trade agreements.*

4—*America's support of collective responsibility for the administration of all colonies and mandates.*

5—*America's support of the principle that higher levels of life and democratic institutions eventually cannot be maintained anywhere unless with their blessings they are made available everywhere.*

6—*America's support of a coalition peace commission representing all political faiths, named by the President, and working with him to create and present this nation's sacrificial program for peace.*

7—*For such a program and with such a program, America's cancellation of war debts.*

And to these seven points there was added still another,—relief to the small democracies, with particular support of the proposed feeding plan for the children and aged of Belgium.

Well, there's a program for you. Young people are sometimes criticized for being long on idealism and short on practice. It's often said that college and high school young people do a lot of day-dreaming about tomorrow's world but that they never come to grips with reality. Dr. Poling's peace platform disposed of that sort of criticism. If the Christian Endeavorers of the United States will push these peace proposals they will be justified years hence in presenting to themselves the Distinguished Service Citation which this year they presented to Governor Stassen. The Convention approved Dr. Poling's peace proposals. The delegates called for American support of a world agency for the administration of world affairs. They gave their okay to the exercising of police power to protect the peace of world government. They advocated open economic frontiers and collective responsibility for the administration of colonies and mandates.

"Some day the war will end," said these young people. "God grant that when the long, hard furrow is ploughed we will be neither too tired, too unprepared, nor too bitter for the task of reconciliation and reconstruction."

I don't know how you feel about it, but to me there's something positively inspiring in the action of these Christian young people at Atlantic City. While the fathers and mothers, or many of them at any rate, are despairing of the future, their sons and daughters are drafting the blueprint of a new world order. If, as their action would seem to indicate, these young people at Atlantic City are prepared to bring the resources of their faith to the task of building a world of justice and of decency, a world in which politics and economics and human relations are brought under the influence of the Carpenter of Nazareth; if these young people are prepared to do that and if they will stick to that purpose, it may well be that this Convention will go down in Christian history as an event of tremendous significance. Now that they've had their say let these young people roll up their sleeves and give this distraught and despairing world a demonstration of Christian young people in action.

Marion Simms and Clifford Earle
Taking a Boardwalk Stroll

IV

President Poling's Message

"Always --- For Christ and the Church"

Address by Dr. Daniel A. Poling, President, at the Thirty-eighth International Christian Endeavor Convention in Atlantic City, New Jersey (July 8-13), given on Wednesday, July 9, 1941

The sixtieth anniversary of the International Society of Christian Endeavor occurs in the hour of declared national emergency and when the world of human affairs rocks upon the brink of social, economic, political, and moral chaos. Thirty years ago we met in this city to celebrate another anniversary. Then the nations were at peace and there was every prospect that peace would continue. Then life moved upon international seas of serenity, though now we know that beneath were boiling tides that would rise to engulf the earth in storms of hatred. These storms continue. There was scarcely an abatement after the armistice of 1918. Now the opening sessions of this sixtieth anniversary convention are lashed with the intensified furies of man's inhumanity to man.

The thirtieth anniversary of Christian Endeavor brought notable guests from many countries and gathered representatives from every state and province of North America. Its program was symbolized by a motto that electrified the nation and captured the imagination of the world. Christian Endeavor's "A saloonless nation by 1920, the three hundredth year from the landing of the Pilgrims at Plymouth," became the rallying call, the forward trumpet of Christian citizenship and civic righteousness. The motto was more than a slogan. In outline it was a program, and before the date named had been reached the goal set had been achieved. Christian Endeavor's slogan was written into the organic law of the land, and America became in 1919 a saloonless nation.

We who gather here for the sixtieth anniversary of Christian Endeavor have witnessed America's great withdrawal. In this convention for many the memories of thirty years ago are clouded by the repeal of the Eighteenth Amendment. Our triumph has been ground into ashes of defeat, and our joy is turned into sorrow. For every saloon of 1911 there are now at least three similar or worse places of liquor sale.

Liquor and the Cigarette

But it is not our purpose to lament and to condole. There is work for us to do. The task now is even greater than was the task of thirty years ago. Christian Endeavor in Atlantic City 1941 declares that Christian youth do not consent to the liquor traffic by whatever name it may be known. Here and now we renew our pledge, rededicate ourselves to the solution of the liquor problem, and here we shall

33

CONVENTION AUDITORIUM

make our plans to contribute our maximum service in the interests of a sober America. The present national emergency makes even more imperative prompt and decisive action. Alcohol has less than nothing to contribute to the national defense. Liquor is a physical, social, and moral menace and unmitigated evil. We as Americans are less than patriotic if we give its traffic for private gain less than its long-merited destruction.

In terms of civic responsibility, the rapidly growing evil of unrestricted cigarette sale and use challenges our attention. Girls as well as boys, women as well as men have become the unrestrained patrons of another traffic that in its present growing development is a serious social menace. We protest the advertising by radio of liquor and of the cigarette. We also protest the advertising in all public media of those commodities that, whatever else may be said about them, are a threat to youth, a serious detriment to the normal development of youth's body and mind. In this convention we would join with all other agencies that have as their common goal the elimination from advertising channels, and particularly from presentation to the whole family, as on the screen and by the radio, of beverage alcohol and of the cigarette.

We commend Allied Youth, child of Christian Endeavor, which, under the leadership of some of the most representative men and women of America, gives today a scientific, statesmanlike program of temperance information and activities to the young people of America. Youth-led—of, by, and for youth—Allied Youth is the most hopeful agency in its field.

Peace in Our Time

Perhaps even more significant and timely than Christian Endeavor's civic slogan of thirty years ago is the motto that may well capture the imagination of this historic gathering,—"Peace in our time." Not appeasement as of Munich; not mediation as of the status quo or in assent to the Dictator's ultimatum; but peace with liberty and justice for all. Certainly such a peace is less than an idle dream while dictators threaten the last defenses of democracy and freedom. First, their evil might must be broken. But already Christian Endeavor has announced the comprehensive, dynamic, and sacrificial program that she will support, the program for which she seeks now the support of the government in Washington; the program that in itself is an objective for youth called into training for the defense of America, a program that in peace or war would be worthily the objective of the American people and that could, we believe, become a trumpet of hope for all the nations of the earth. Only a few weeks ago the Northern Baptist Convention adopted this program in principle and instructed its Permanent Commission to implement the recommendations. These principles are:

1. *America's support of a world agency for the administration of world affairs, —this without interference with purely internal affairs.* In other words, the application of the Federal principle internationally.

2. *America's support of police power for such an administration of world affairs.* Theodore Roosevelt, in his Nobel Prize address in 1910, advocated a league of nations, backed by an international armed force, to keep the "peace of righteousness." He said: "The policeman must be put back of the judge in international law, just as he is back of the judge in municipal law. The effective power of civilization must be put back of civilization's collective purpose to secure reasonable justice between nation and nation."

3. *America's support of open economic frontiers, with free access to raw materials and natural resources, and with reciprocal trade agreements.* So long as there is economic control by the "haves" against the "have-nots," the economic causes for armed conflict remain.

4. *America's support of collective responsibility for the administration of all colonies and mandates.* Collective responsibility should everywhere be substituted for national ownership. This would not affect dominions within empires, for dominions are free and sovereign states within the empires of their choice.

5. *America's support of the principle that higher levels of life and democratic institutions eventually cannot be maintained anywhere unless with their blessings they are made available everywhere.* One man cannot hold another down without staying with him. The principle is universal. Also, it is the Christian ethic. "I am my brother's keeper." Also, that ethic applies at last within nations and to international affairs.

6. *America's support of a coalition peace commission representing all political faiths, named by the President, and working with him to create and present this nation's sacrificial program for peace.*

7. *Finally, for such a program and with such a program, America's cancellation of war debts.*

"Peace in our time" is thus the goal of Christian Endeavor. "Peace in our time" is the objective of our Christian citizenship. As we give our sympathy, our practical support, our utmost assistance, whatever eventually that may involve, to the struggling democracies that are today America's first line of defense, "peace in our time" is the goal. As from this convention we reach our hands across the sea to our comrades in Britain, and to the friends of freedom under all flags however low the tragedy of dictatorship may have brought them, "peace in our time" is the goal. The clasp of friendship is doubly strong because its hand is the hand of constructive, dynamic, sacrificial peace, —"peace in our time."

Other men and women of good will who are of our spiritual company are proponents of "Union Now." Essentially Christian Endeavor's peace formula is at harmony with "Union Now." In principle, these two agree. Each and both are inclusive and not exclusive. Each and both open the door to the eventual solidarity and unity of all who would be free. Neither black nor white, nor German, nor Italian, nor English, nor American shall be excluded in that new era which, under God, shall be the era of the soul—that new world order of democracy as of the Bill of Rights, and of liberty with law.

Americans All

Let this new world order begin in America and in our hearts. Surely, this is the land where hate should die. Intolerance—intolerance of color, faith, or race—in a democracy, is the greatest social sin. If America would be strong, if her defenses, physical, moral and spiritual, are to be adequate, then we must be "Americans All." Without prejudice to our individual loyalties and, indeed, strengthening every worthy loyalty, we must be "Americans All." Black and white, Protestant, Catholic and Jew, now and forever, we must be "Americans All"!

The Voice of Conscience

A major issue of Christian character rises now for those who must reconcile participation in any war or preparation for any war with Christian life and testimony. Does not following Christ require that men should be conscientious objectors? Is not pacifism identical with Christianity? But Christians do respond to the call of country; they have gone and are now going to the colors. Or are they merely bearers of His name and not doers of His word? What should we say of these things?

For hundreds of thousands the issue is now tragically drawn. Christian Endeavorers are facing the issue and searching us for the answer. Some are conscientious objectors. They have signed the register of their church, and in every church there should be a register for conscientious objectors. The church must follow through with each of these. Each must have her comfort and guidance. Wherever men and women in the line of duty may go, wherever faithful to conscience and loyal to Christ they are found, the church must companion them. The church must be the church.

But what of these others, the overwhelming number? Let there be no evasion of the issue. By all the tests I know, they have accepted Christ and He has accepted them. "Whatsoever He saith unto thee, do it," is the trumpet of their souls. They are doing now what they have heard Him "say." His relationships with men are as individual and personal as that command, which is also, and perhaps chiefly, an invitation.

No, to be Christian it is not necessary to be a conscientious objector. I believe that the conscientious objector has a major contribution to make to the righteous and Christian world order. I am proud of my country because of the recognition of the status of the conscientious objector in the new draft law. But, generally, those pre-eminent Christians whom I have known in the years of my public ministry have not been conscientious objectors. But they have loved their enemies. They have done good to those who hated them. They have kept His faith. That conscientious objectors recognize the Christian validity of those who differ with them in the application of Christian faith to the present world crisis is revealed in a recent letter from English Friends to the Philadelphia Meeting of Friends: "We are bound to refuse, at no matter what cost, all that conflicts with our loyalty to Christ. Yet, strongly as we hold to our Christian peace testimony, we cannot separate ourselves from the nation of which we are a part and to which we owe so much. Let us not fail of understanding and respect for those who are risking all in response to the call to arms."

"England's Hour," by Vera Brittain, is a small volume made up of letters from people in every walk of life under the brutal fire of war. From one letter she quotes: "England cannot watch its holiest monuments being battered, with system and pre-meditation, and then meet the enemy afterward in a forgiving, tolerant spirit." "Can it not?" asks Miss Brittain; and this is her rejoinder: "If not, then it has already lost the peace; and if it loses yet another peace, the war of 1965 will annihilate our children and our London, too." The woman who wrote that is not a conscientious objector.

Nor shall I ever forget the closing sentence of a letter from a friend in Germany, a letter received on the day troops crossed into Poland: "Whatever happens to our bodies, our hearts are yours forever." The man who wrote that is not a conscientious objector.

Recently I received a letter from a young woman, a graduate student in a state university. In the letter were these sentences: "What does this word 'love' really mean —'love your enemies'? As we too often interpret it, is it not outworn, unrealistic, taken for granted? What does it mean in our personal life? Well, I have come to the conclusion that it means action, that this 'love your enemies' is an active love. This

other, this nice, comfortable, secure feeling that is usually called 'love' just won't do
—now." The young woman who wrote this is not a conscientious objector.

"Love your enemies . . . . do good to them that hate you" . . . . "Whatsoever He saith unto you, do it!"

Christian Endeavor World Emergency

The President of the United States has declared a state of complete national emergency. This sixtieth anniversary Christian Endeavor Convention assembles in a state of Christian Endeavor world emergency. But our world emergency, under God, is *world opportunity*. New occasions teach new duties, and equally they require new programs, new leadership, and a renewed dedication to the unfinished task. Your trustees have adopted the recommendation of your Executive Committee and President that in this world emergency Christian Endeavor activities be centered in one organization, given one leadership; that organizationally a new, vital, comprehensive unity be achieved.

The International Society has requested the World's Christian Endeavor Union to function in all areas, through all departments, in all nations, and with utmost sacrifice and speed. This Convention becomes essentially a world's program, a world program for restoration and advance. Our gifts and our service are now the vital support of Christian Endeavor at home and abroad and without discrimination.

With the motto, "Always—For Christ and the Church," we launch here a complete program for individuals and societies, for local, state, and national unions. The program in all its particulars will be released through our conferences and from this Convention throughout all our relationships. At a suitable time, you shall be invited to join this world advance with gifts and with pledges and with enlistment to secure additional funds.

I have been shamed by the living faith, by the demonstrated loyalty of our British associates. Their headquarters under London skies is a mass of rubble. Their physical properties have all been destroyed, but in not one element has Christian Endeavor ceased to function and from not a single leader comes the voice of despair. Rather, when my first suggestion for a restoration fund reached England, the first reply came from a former British Christian Endeavor Union president and it was a pledge of two pounds, or ten dollars, for the fund.

Christian Endeavor World Opportunity

Between now and January first, unless Christian Endeavor in America fails utterly, we shall reach our sixtieth anniversary goal of $60,000. With the birthday of Mother Clark as the rallying point we shall gather our funds, making sure not only the restoration but the intensifying and the expansion of Christian Endeavor—in America? Yes! But also throughout Europe and Asia, across India and to the last islands of the seas.

This Convention has many voices but, thank God, one voice is missing—the voice of defeat. This Convention has many problems. Thank God for the problems! This Convention has a multitude of tasks, and not one of these shall be declined. And this Convention has youth—youth for Christ and for the Church—always.

The sixtieth anniversary Christian Endeavor Convention has an open door and, God helping us, we shall enter and possess our heritage of peace and power. There is no room here for weaklings, no time here for compromise. For Christ and for the Church we stir ourselves from the failures we confess, from the delays that shame us, and standing at the "ready" we lift the united voice, "Speak, Lord, for thy servant heareth."

Now may I stop long enough to hear with you the voices from many lands, and as you listen you will know that behind these representatives who are present are scores and even hundreds of others who would have messages equally significant were they able to be present. These others are thwarted by distance or poverty or war. We have had practically no correspondence from the Continent of Europe since troops crossed the Polish frontier on September 1, 1939, but in the Balkans and in Baltic countries, in Scandinavian lands, in Germany, Italy, Spain, Portugal, France, and Hungary Christian Endeavor is not dead. Our comrades, separated from us by frontiers that momentarily are impassable, are bound to us and we are bound to them with ties of love that shall not be severed. And now the voices:

[At this point Dr. Poling paused and the lights were dimmed. With a spotlight picking out speaker after speaker, a number of young people, each representing a particular country, brought new word of Christian Endeavor.]

Messages from Representative Countries

Around the World

Asia

China   "Under the conditions since the war, Christian Endeavor has maintained and strengthened its position. In the occupied area most of the societies are continuing their work, and with increased opportunities for evangelism. In West China our work never was in better condition. Twelve hundred societies are on our records. Twenty thousand copies of the 1941 topic books have been distributed. Two hundred new societies have been organized in two years."

India   India, including India, Burma and Ceylon, has now 2,000 societies, the number being augmented two years ago by the merger of all the Epworth Leagues of the Methodist Church. This merger brought 50,000 new Endeavorers into the national and world-wide fellowship. Under the leadership of the Abbeys—Vere and Jessie—the union has strengthened its denominational ties, and the day is not far distant when India may give a complete demonstration of cooperation in young people's work for Christ and the Church.

Japan   "Whatever may be the final form of our union in connection with the new structure of the churches in Japan, we shall keep our historical Christian fellowship with the World's Christian Endeavor Union."

Korea   "The governmental pressure which dissolved our national union three years ago has made the work of our 2,000 societies very weak. But the spirit of Christian Endeavor still lives on in the hearts of thousands of Koreans who love Christ and His cause, and who greet you in His name."

Africa

South Africa   Twenty district unions, more than 400 young people's societies,
(Dutch Church)   and 800 children's societies make an effective work for Christ in South Africa. Missionary work and hospital work are especially strong.

Egypt   The ancient land of Egypt maintains more than a hundred Christian Endeavor societies, most of them under the supervision of the missions and schools scattered throughout the Nile Valley.

Australia

Australia   Since the World's Convention in 1938, there has been a constant upward trend in Christian Endeavor in all the states on the Australian continent. The movement is characterized by an intense loyalty to Christ and to the social responsibilities of the gospel. More than 100,000 members are now enrolled and active in more than 4,000 societies.

Central America

Nicaragua   "At the last national convention one group of Endeavorers traveled nine days to reach the meeting. Conferences, Bible study, addresses, personal testimony, and a communion service were features. All felt the nearness of God and the oneness of His people—Miskitoes, Sumus, Creoles, Americans, all communing together."

Mexico "In May the Mexican Union had a very successful national convention in Monterrey. We are making progress, and look forward to the day when our union can be a full-fledged and serving member in the family of the World's Christian Endeavor Union."

Islands

Trinidad, British West Indies "In April the Canadian Mission Church (under the United Church of Canada) celebrated fifty years of Christian Endeavor. In nearly every district we have a Christian Endeavor society. Our union takes in also Baptist and American Methodist societies."

Samoan Islands "Christian Endeavor was introduced to the islands fifty years ago, and it has spread to every village and is established in every island. Our meetings began with a Christian Endeavor rally, which really knocked the spots off anything I have ever seen in England. The Samoans love ceremony, and they came streaming along the road, from the port twelve miles away, in thousands, complete with bands and banners."

South America

Venezuela Christian Endeavor societies are used as a means of evangelizing young people in nearby districts, by means of public meetings, the distribution of evangelistic literature, and by personal work. New young people are continually finding their way to Christ and into Christian work.

Europe

Holland "Since our meetings can be held only in daylight hours, we can get along much better in summer than in winter. We pray for the end of the war."

Hungary "On the whole, a growing interest for the Christian Endeavor movement and for the earnest gospel message can be noticed all over the country. The annual convention brought together a large number of delegations when only a few were expected because of the troublesome times."

Jugoslavia "The last annual conference proved that God's word is still a strong magnet attracting young people."

Latvia "Passing into the new year, our prayer is to hold out on our lonely watch. We send the most heartfelt greetings to all God's children. May God bless and succeed the Christian Endeavor movement everywhere."

Italy "Our young people go on strongly. The movement belongs now to the Church and is solid and progressing. It is a *blessing* for our Church."

Norway "Last November the national convention was held with good representation. The principal work of the union is to win the youth for Christ and the Church and the new officers will press toward this end."

Poland "Most of our meetings continue; the brothers and sisters assemble gladly, even though many of them are uprooted and dispersed."

Germany The magazine, *Entschiedenes Christentum*, continues to tell of activities in societies and unions, with evangelism always in chief place of emphasis. More than 1,500 societies were in the records up to the opening of the war.

Great Britain   Blackouts, bombings, and evacuations have in no sense put Christian Endeavor to rout in the British Isles. The head-quarters and supply house in London fell a victim to bombing in December and were completely destroyed; the annual convention could not be held in May, 1941; but the cause still prevails and as the leaders say, "We will go forward."

[Dr. Poling resumed]

An Hour Sublime

One of our most distinguished guests, Dr. Adolph Keller, told us of the invisible body of Christ that even now rises in the souls of the peoples of nations where formal worship has been liquidated, where church buildings have been leveled, and where the clergy have been slain or silenced. He tells us that Christian Endeavor, unique in its attributes, has and will have a unique opportunity to begin at the first possible moment a spiritual invasion of those areas now swept by mechanized, destructive might. Never has there been a time when Christian youth faced so imperative a world task, so great an ordeal, an hour so sublime.

And what shall we say of America? All that has been said of overseas opportunity we direct now to these, our own United States, and Canada. The World's Christian Endeavor Union, functioning as never before in North America, will continue and intensify the relationships between Christian Endeavor and the denominations and with all other religious and patriotic bodies. Christian Endeavor is and has been for sixty years ecumenical. Christian Endeavor is today the ecumenical youth movement of the ecumenical church. Our program-building agencies, with the direction of the World's Union and with the executive leadership so thoroughly tried over a long decade, will maintain the Educational Council, create the topics and offer every acceptable and available support to the states and provinces and to the individual churches and societies. The next great continental convention and perhaps regional conferences as well will receive the special attention of the World's Union Executive Committee. Your President has already outlined plans for his maximum service in the trust to which he has been called.

But One and One alone is our High Command. This is a *Christian* Endeavor Society. Always "For Christ and the Church" is its purpose and always Jesus Christ Himself is our Redeemer, our Comrade and Captain. Christian Endeavor is not just another youth club. Its covenant pledge, its place within the church, its evangelical faith and loyalty, its evangelistic fervor, its missionary commitment, its sense of civic obligation, its patriotism, its international spirit, and its incomparable genius for Christian fellowship, make it today the transcendent youth agency of our living, universal faith. In this faith we accept our high commission and press toward the goal of peace in our time—the peace that passeth all understanding, that is in Jesus Christ our Lord.

V

"We Count On You"

"World Reporters" Speak

THERE was more than urgency in the voices of some of the men and
women who spoke from the Convention platform in these history-
making July days and nights. There was almost the undertone of des-
peration, as men and women told young people what goes on in the world
in 1941, with no effort to make the picture pretty and appealing.

In these stark and terrible portrayals of what is happening in other
lands today, the keen-eyed observers who had thought so deeply on world
problems held out only one hope.

It was expressed clearly by every speaker who presented the world
picture to the Convention. It could be put into these words:

*The youth of other lands have a burning, sacrificial faith in the
dreams of their leaders. Christian youth can help the world only by car-
ing to live—and if need be, die—in an even greater spirit of sacrifice
than the young people who are following the dictators.*

Those who listened to Dr. Gezork, to Edwin Espy and Joy Homer, to
Philip Lee and the others, realized clearly that if Christianity has any
meaning to them they must act—and now—to prove their faith.

"We Bring a Challenge"

Such speakers as they came to this Convention from other lands, indeed, from other ages of man, and had not come to entertain or divert
the delegates. Into their words and their voices came the earnestness of
messengers who bring a challenge. Their task, they were certain, was
to make Christian youth aware of a tremendous crisis in world history.

Some would say, "A word like *challenge* has been worn smooth with
too much handling." Gezork, Espy, Miss Homer, and others re-minted
that word.

Philip Lee and Vere Abbey spoke from their warm, intimate knowledge of Asia. Here Christianity triumphs day upon day—Lee knew
this for China, Vere Abbey for India. *Yet these triumphs only emphasize the tremendous advances still to be made.*

41

Dr. Herbert Gezork, who not long ago was General Secretary of the Baptist Youth Union in Germany, laid heavy duties at the doorstep of American Christian youth, for some of the events that came to Germany can happen here! Nazi agents think of themselves as missionaries of a faith. Communists believe it is their mission to save the world. And the pathway to youth's heart has been left wide open for the entrance and progress of the emissaries of class hatred and anti-Christian doctrines, through the lassitude of young people who have a higher belief but work at it infrequently.

"Is There Hope for Christian Youth?" was the arresting title that R. H. Edwin Espy, General Secretary of the Student Volunteer Movement, chose for his message to the Convention.

Joy Homer's challenge from China was just as pointed.

Dr. Adolph Keller insisted, "Christian youth has to share the hunger and poverty sweeping over a continent."

But we are keeping you from first-hand acquaintance with the men and women who did so much to make the Atlantic City Convention memorable as "a sweeping panorama of what the new generation of Christians has before it, in the way of challenges and possibilities." "Always—For Christ and the Church" was now seen as a holy affirmation such as men may make at the point of a sword.

The Fate of Europe

A Challenge to America's Christian Youth

From an Address by

DR. HERBERT GEZORK

Assistant Professor of Biblical History at Wellesley College and of Social Ethics at Andover-Newton Theological Seminary; Former General Secretary of the Baptist Youth Union in Germany

It is with deep emotion that I stand before you tonight and look into these young faces. The sight brings memories of happier days when we in Europe worked in our Christian Youth Movement. I remember when I hiked with American, English and Czech Christians over the mountains of Czechoslovakia. Where is Czechoslovakia tonight? I remember other happy days when we bicycled along the dykes of Holland. Where is Holland tonight? I remember when we canoed along the Vistula—and where is Poland tonight?

Where are these young men of Europe? They are in dreadful bombers, in submarines, on bloody battlefields across Europe, in concentration camps, in dark graves. You can understand my emotion when I think of the end of Christian work—its leaders in concentration camps, driven out of their country, silenced in other ways.

DR. HERBERT GEZORK, Europe

MISS JOY HOMER, China

REV. VERE W. ABBEY, India

DR. ADOLPH KELLER, Europe

I have another message to bear—a message that Hitler taught me. It is a warning lesson and a challenge to Christian youth.

I am uncompromisingly opposed to all that Hitler stands for. I regard it as a dreadful manifestation of paganism in these days. Yet I see some things as I look back upon those dreadful days. I see lessons we German youth of yesterday had not learned. I can give them as my warning to you.

I returned to Germany in 1931 from a two-year trip around the world. I was eager to get into contact again with the trends of thinking among Germany's youth.

A Contrast That Lives in Memory

Two evenings stand out in my memory of that time. The one was a meeting of young people, mostly intellectuals, who came together to discuss their problems. The air was thick with the smoke of many cigarettes and with the fog of many questions.

But it seemed this group had no answers. Indeed, it seemed these young people did not particularly want to find answers. They seemed well satisfied with turning their problems over and over. For they were disillusioned, sophisticated, cynical. All was relative to them.

A few evenings later I attended a meeting of Hitler Youth. Everything was different. Here was faith, here was commitment. These young people had an ideal and believed frantically in it. They had dedicated themselves to it.

Theirs was a terrible ideal, to me, but they stood unflinchingly for it. That evening I began to fear for the future of Germany. These were so sure, the other young people were so doubtful. And two years later Hitler won.

The lesson for us in this experience is evident. If, as a university president in this country has said, the youth of America are primarily interested in having a good time and if, as recently a leading commentator wrote, our youth are permeated with the spirit of a sophisticated cynicism, then the danger is here. Some faith—and it might be an evil, destructive faith—might conquer America, as it has conquered in Germany.

The Human Soul Longs for Certainty

When you throw out faith in Jesus Christ some ugly, destructive faith comes in. The human soul must have something to hold to—the God of Jesus or the god of Stalin and Hitler. You have a chance to give to your country the highest cause in faith and dedication—the cause of Jesus Christ.

Let me share with you another thought. I will talk about missionary work. Do you know which two cities have been, during the past years, the greatest fountain-heads of missionary activity? These cities are Moscow and Berlin.

We may call the men and women who have gone out from there to win adherents to their faith and to pave the way for the victory of their cause Fifth Columnists or subversive agents.

But they think of themselves as missionaries of a faith which is destined to win the world.

Have we Christians not lost this missionary zeal, this fervor to win followers for our Cause, the greatest cause that ever was—the Kingdom of God? Do we really think that we can beat that missionary zeal of Nazis and Communists by sitting back in our chairs, singing hymns, and letting the world go by?

In college I watched the Communist and Nazi students going from group to group, talking. I saw that again and again they were successful.

In North Germany on another occasion, two young girls came into the train. For days they had gone from farm to farm to talk with the people. The farmers and their wives were being propagandized for Hitler. The girls had been chased with dogs from some of the farms. It was cold, they didn't need to do this work, they came from comfortable homes—but they were missionaries for a cause.

Any church which does not believe in missions becomes an empty shell. The churches of Europe became too interested in themselves as institutions. They were not interested in going out in missionary effort. In Russia in 1917, at the beginning of the Bolshevist Revolution, the priests were discussing what color of robe a priest should wear in the services. The storm came and swept them away.

For Results, Sacrifice

And there is a third thought that the rise of Hitlerism has impressed indelibly upon my mind—that no cause can conquer for which no sacrifices are made.

I remember the young Nazi who lived in the house next to mine in Berlin. That was an anti-Nazi neighborhood, and those were violent days in which the Hitler party fought its way to power. Each time this young man went into the street at night he risked his life. Many times he was beaten severely by political opponents. More than once he came home with his face streaming with blood. And yet, whenever I argued with him, whenever his mother implored him to give up his party allegiance, he always had the answer: "This is my cause. In this I believe. For this I shall gladly die if necessary."

What a challenge to us, Christian youth! Let us not forget that the blood of the martyrs was the seed of the Church of Christ. Let us not forget that we claim to follow a Man who died on a cross. Let us not forget that whoever wants to be His disciple must take His cross upon himself. I have no fear for the Cause of Christ, but I sometimes fear for us. Perhaps we have lost that heroic, sacrificial spirit that made the early Christians go to their death with songs on their lips, that sent Livingstone into the darkest Africa, that sent Father Damien to the lepers of Hawaii, that sent Kagawa into the slums of Kobe.

When I hear what people today call sacrifice, I can only wonder, as I remember what other people are sacrificing for their causes.

I do not fear for the Cause of Jesus in the future, but I feel that America may have to go through the same terrible experiences as Europe, unless we regain the spirit of sacrifice for and commitment to the Cause of Jesus.

The word of Jesus comes back to me again and again—"What do you more than others?" The youth of Communism and Nazism—what do you more than they?

On your answer, not in words but in lives, depends the future of America and of the world. May we all be strengthened to answer, as in the hymn we sing so often, "Lord, we are able!"

Something in China Amazed Her

Joy Homer, daughter of the famous operatic star, Louise Homer, and of Sidney Homer, eminent composer, went to China as a newspaper correspondent. She did not expect to "cover" religion. She did not expect to be impressed by the work of the Christian missionaries nor won to admiration for Christian leadership in China.

Her testimony in the International Christian Endeavor Convention and in other places has been all the more striking because she had not planned to look for Christian influences in the bombed and suffering land of this great and patient people.

Joy Homer is young, as her hearers were young. She seemed hardly more "aged" than a university undergraduate. Brisk, staccato delivery of her message, which was given without notes, helped to make it one of the most impressive that graced a Convention which grew hourly in the stature and significance of its affirmations on Christian living.

China, As I Saw It

From an Address by

JOY HOMER

There was a time—about a million years ago, I guess—when Chungking wasn't being bombed. That was when I arrived there the first time. About three days after I arrived the first raid came.

Beyond the porch of the house where I stayed there was a sand-bar, on which a happy old man lived in a little straw hut or mat shed. Thirty-five bombs fell on the sand-bar. The mat shed disappeared. I saw the old man lying still and thought him dead. After the raid I went out to do some rescue work. And there was the mat shed! The old man was putting some finishing touches on its roof. Before I left he was sitting down in comfort. That's China.

At a place where houses had been burned out for half a mile I saw men digging. I asked what they were doing.

"Putting in a water-main," they replied.

"You're crazy!" I said. "All the houses have gone."

"This," said they, "is for the houses we'll be putting up next month."

Odd place, this free China! I arrived there when Canton had just fallen. Now was the time, they thought, to clean out the corruption of several million aeons and build a new China. Right now, with a war going on, was the time to establish new libraries, social reforms, schools! For China is a boom country, a jubilant country. Its people haven't lost their sense of humor nor their nonchalant love of life.

Shortcut—Through a Battle

A donkey-cart driver, taking me to a certain place, went on the road leading directly through a battle. Because it was a shortcut, you see.

Machinery for the new industrial cities of the West was taken piece by piece from Shanghai by coolies!

More surprising than the reconstruction under bomb-fire is the strange spirit of the Chinese, something more than tolerance. Ask them what they think of the Japanese, and they reply, "We're fighting the military until we drive them out, but not the Japanese people."

"The Japanese people are not to blame," they insist. "They're our neighbors and sometime we'll make them our friends."

I saw a Japanese sergeant taken prisoner. A little later I heard laughter and went to see what was happening. There were twenty or thirty little Chinese soldiers about, and in the center of the group this Japanese soldier was teaching them wrestling tricks. The next day he was hero of the camp.

American-Educated Youth at Work

Then there are the young people of China, the students who walked with their equipment on their backs some three thousand miles. Young people, these, who had never picked up a pin for themselves until China's crisis came. Sometimes they took the professors and held classes when they tired of walking. They were bombed. They were hungry. They laughed, though, to see which of their professors could lecture without their notes!

The American-educated youth of China are running their country.

There was a student dying outside a Japanese-held city. He said that he had come back to that city from the West to get a microscope, which he knew was in his old college laboratory.

"We needed it in our new college," he said simply. "I got it. It's being taken on by a friend. They shot me but I got our microscope."

A girl of sixteen who had been doing relief work and who lost an arm and a leg from injuries in an air-raid said this:

"It isn't too terrible. We didn't come to die, we came to help China—but we came to die if we must."

For the first time in her history the masses of China are being educated. Young people are teaching the soldiers to read and write. The soldiers learn their lessons on the long marches. They pin their lessons on the back of the soldier in front of them, and learn it as they march!

I saw an Arts College where the students were living in caves in a cliff. Their quarters made you think of a terraced skyscraper. These students were rehearsing an opera they had composed. It was wonderfully good. There was a chorus of eighty or ninety, and an orchestra.

That is China—fighting a war with one hand and with the other pulling herself up out of decadence.

Meet the Missionaries!

The missionaries? They are quite a crowd. You find them heading up relief work, starting schools, building highways with relief labor, starting cooperatives so that China can support herself.

More important even than saving lives, China is seeing Christianity not preached, but working! Christianity has become the religion of the country. It's not the lukewarm kind we turn off and on like a faucet.

Practical people, the Chinese. Not interested in creeds. They want to know how this young man Jesus teaches men to live. This Jesus-way is getting new roots in China, making these people strong as steel.

A little coolie explained it all—by accident.

Chungking, a cliff city, has only one entrance. It was a death-trap in the early days. When the bombs came there were mile-long fires, engulfing whole blocks. The people couldn't move fast in the narrow streets and they were burned alive. In the ruins the wounded screamed for help.

In such a time someone yelled, "There's the Generalissimo and Madame Chiang!" There they were indeed, hand in hand, tired, dirty, close to tears. The crowd noticed that they had no bodyguard and there was a touch of panic.

"They'll be killed," some of the people cried.

Then a little boy silenced the panic. "It's all right," he said. "They've got Jesus."

Dr. Gezork and Miss Homer were the featured speakers of the Thursday evening meeting of the Rainbow Jubilee Convention. Mrs. Helen Lyon Jones, Vice-President of the International Society, presided at this session and Alvin Stevens of Baltimore, Maryland, led the period of worship.

Those Other "Foreign Reports"

In the daytime sessions Christian Endeavor's other messengers from the distant strands were heard by attentive audiences.

The paragraphs that follow, to make this one of the most important chapters in the Atlantic City Convention's chronicles, give the gist of international messages that fitted into the Convention schedule in this manner:

Wednesday morning, Dr. Adolph Keller, of Geneva, Switzerland.

Thursday morning, Rev. Philip Lee, of Shanghai, China.

Friday, official banquet, R. H. Edwin Espy, General Secretary of the Student Volunteer Movement.

Sunday afternoon, Rev. Vere W. Abbey, of India.

What Christian Youth Faces in Europe

From an Address by

DR. ADOLPH KELLER

of Geneva, Switzerland. Secretary, Central Bureau for Relief of the Evangelical Churches of Europe

There is no time to speak of the tragedy of children in Spain and Greece and Belgium, who without knowing what is coming face starvation. Or of those children in Finland who during the last winter could not go to school or Sunday school except by shifts, because there were not clothes enough for all. Nor of the French boys whose fathers are prisoners in German camps.

Many may be fortunate enough to live in blessed ignorance about their future, but others know that they may be marked by the dark and terrible angel, and die in their youth.

What a sinister vision for those who have eyes to see what they may have to face in the near future! And what gratitude toward God must this vision awake in you, for being allowed to have a happy and unmenaced youth!

Christian youth has to share the hunger and poverty sweeping over a continent. Many young people in Europe may ask, "Is it worth-while to struggle? to pray? to believe in a God of love in a world of horror?"

What Shall Youth Expect?

Uncertainty about the future, about the value of faith, is the spiritual climate in which millions must dwell today. Youth have to share this uncertainty as they have to share hunger and persecution, trying to keep faith in a God whom they can no longer understand. The greatest task of Christian parents and leaders living in such conditions is to try to inspire young people with a faith which is as sure as that of the Psalmist, "Though I make my bed in hell, God is there also."

The boys of Pastor Niemoeller, seeing how their father has suffered for three years in a concentration camp, understand that Christians in today's world may have to carry a cross like our Master, and yet not despair. There are boys and girls in France going through an amazing apprenticeship of suffering. A spiritual harvest is opening in millions of young souls, a harvest of suffering and self-denial, far richer than that of youth just out for a good time and having no sense of duty and heroism.

Ideas Coming Out of Totalitarianism

There are more concrete problems of today, that Christian youth have to face in Europe. There is a new educational system, in which they are helplessly enmeshed. It is diametrically opposed to the Christian spirit. The ideas placed before them no longer come from above, but rise from below—ideas of force and of racial and nationalistic doctrine.

Some may ask, "Is it not better for youth to belong to the State, to be disciplined and physically fit, than to tramp the roads in hunger, in armies of crime, as they did in Russia after the last war?"

The dictators, some will say, have won the enthusiasm of youth. What has Christianity done to inspire a similar enthusiasm? Has the church ever kindled such a fire in young Christians, and made them willing in heart and soul to serve the cause of their Master, Jesus?

Rosenberg, the minister of education in Germany, says, "Christians only *sing* 'Onward, Christian soldiers, marching as to war,' while we, the strong, disciplined disciples of the nationalistic ideal, really march! We fight, while others are singing and praying and cultivating sweet inner feelings. We conquer the world!"

Christian youth are not going to fight for the victory of Christ. The church, however, must meet these three conditions:

I

The church must present Christ to youth not as a weakling, a sentimental or romantic preaching pilgrim, a moralist, social reformer, or idealist—but as the Son of God who is challenging our whole being as nobody else does!

II

The youth of the church can expect to be a minority. They must not be hypnotized by large crowds, majority standing, and quick and easy victories. Forget the superstitious belief in the big, the superlative, the large armies of those who do not make decisions.

III

We must awaken a new missionary and evangelistic spirit in Christianity. Europe will become a great mission field when the human heart will have emptied itself of all the horrible things filling it today. A new hunger, a new thirst, for the gospel is already evident. This does not mean that we need an American crusade to Americanize Europe, but it means that Europe will need thousands of hearts and hands to rebuild what is destroyed—homes, chapels, churches, youth hostels, and human hopes.

Europe will need thousands who are willing to live with the poor, the abandoned, the discouraged, to share their suffering and strengthen their faith in the love of God and of their brethren and in a better world

If the contribution of European Christianity toward the coming church of Christ will be deep, spiritual experiences, ripening in the present time of suffering and hardship, the contribution of American youth may be inner preparedness to share the experiences of the churches under the Cross, new willingness to understand, and dynamic, sacrificial faith which will enable America to be the Good Samaritan of the world.

Rev. Philip Lee, of the China Christian Broadcasting Association, Shanghai, China, was one of the most popular leaders in the Convention. His gracious manner and his willingness to cooperate in every possible way to assure the success of the Convention endeared him to every last delegate. Mr. Lee possesses a glorious singing voice, which was particularly beautiful when he sang "The Lord's Prayer" in the pageant, "For Christ and the Church," on Saturday evening.

In his brief but expressive message to Atlantic City 1941, Mr. Lee conveyed first the greetings of Rev. Alfred T. Y. Chow, General Secretary of the China Christian Endeavor Union, and of all Chinese Endeavorers. He then spoke thoughtfully and earnestly of what Christ means to China in a crisis which his fellow Christians there "are at work to turn into the great opportunity of service."

What Christian Youth Faces in the Orient

From an Address by

REV. PHILIP LEE

The Christian youth of China, along with the people of China as a whole, have been going through four years of tremendous suffering. Fifty millions have been made refugees. Among these many are young people. The reports you hear and see through the press are but a tenth of what the actual situation is. More than physical suffering is involved; the people have the anguish of seeing the wonderful accomplishments of the new China Republic being blown into a thousand bits.

However, they are not discouraged. They are carrying on. Those students whose campuses have been wrecked have been moved to the interior. Most of them marched on foot day by day, having classes along the migration when they rested awhile. However the difficulties in carrying on are enormous. Food is scarce, students are without support from their families. Therefore they need your assistance.

Along with the hardships, the Christian youth of China are facing the greatest opportunity of building a new China. For the first time they see their country of 450 million souls being united. They see China by sheer will to live becoming able to defy a military power. They see the vast resources in the West ready to be used. More than that, they see their nation in the midst of the shifting sands of time, groping for a foundation on which to build their nation, seeking the opportunity of setting her upon the Rock of Ages which is Jesus Christ.

Today Christian youth are at work to turn this crisis into the great opportunity of service. Those who are in schools are studying in the forenoon and going out each afternoon to conduct mass educational classes along the streets and in the temples. Graduates of Christian colleges are being asked by the government to organize industrial cooperatives to rehabilitate refugees. Through their individual and collective Christian living they are the greatest testimonies among the people.

"Know Christianity" Movement

In the schools all over China there is a movement which is taking hold of students. It is called the "Know Christianity" movement, to meet the earnest search for truth of non-Christian students. China as a people is witnessing Christianity at work, not only through the heroic missionaries who stayed by them through the war, but through the native Christian leaders of all walks of life. For most of the leaders of Free China today are Christian men and women, products of mission work. At the head of the government are the two most outstanding Christians of this generation, General and Madame Chiang Kai-shek. Then five of the members of the cabinet are Christians. In the "Who's Who" of China, 58 per cent are Christians. These are leading China out of superstitions and idol worship into the knowledge of God.

Young people of China are looking to you as their big brothers and sisters. They are very keen in observing what you do and what you think, because you have given them the light through the missionaries you sent. Since most of our young people's work in the churches is organized as Christian Endeavor societies, you can do a great deal in helping them through your interest in them and your support of the local work. China will be a new nation after the war. We are looking for a way of life to create new individuals and thus a new nation.

The world is in a transitional period again. It is like a symphonic piece, passing from one movement into another. There are harsh notes and unharmonic chords. In our hands is the opportunity to modulate this into a perfect cadence.

Rev. and Mrs. Vere W. Abbey and others
marching in the Boardwalk parade

Of Youth in Troubled Europe

R. H. Edwin Espy, General Secretary of the Student Volunteer Movement, speaking informally at the Convention Banquet, gave from his years of experience with Europe's young people many illustrations of the zeal of Communist and Nazi youth.

He told of an attractive, keen-minded young man with whom he roomed at Heidelberg University. This young student was a Nazi who particularly admired a professor under whom he had taken several semesters' work. One day the student discovered that his professor had one Jewish grandparent—was one-fourth Jewish, according to Nazi measurements.

"My heart and mind are pulling against each other," the young man told Mr. Espy. "I love this professor, but my duty calls me to denounce him as a Jew. I shall lose credit for all the work I have taken under him and he will be dismissed from the University."

In spite of Mr. Espy's pleading that in this case the heart should rule, the student took his stand before the professor's classroom the next day, and informed all the students of his discovery. Not one student entered the classroom and soon afterward the professor was obliged to resign.

"Is there hope for Christian youth? No, unless they have more faith than those whose religion is Communism or Nazism," said Mr. Espy.

That there are zealous Christians among the youth of Europe was also shown by Mr. Espy. In Estonia he found that young people are teaching the principles of Jesus in spite of the wishes and regulations of the government. Frequently the young people who teach Christianity disappear and are not heard of again.

In a camp of young people in France, Mr. Espy asked, "What are you going to do in the future?" Most of the young people answered: "We have no future. Our lives are at the mercy of forces we cannot control."

But one girl replied, "We have a future as we have a past. We are a part of the great heritage of Christianity. *We shall hold fast to our faith.*"

A Meeting-Place of Christian Workers

In his Sunday afternoon address, coming toward the close of the Convention, Rev. Vere W. Abbey spoke for India's Christians and her vast opportunities for advance in heart-warming terms.

Young people expressed great interest in what Mr. Abbey told so modestly of the uniting of Protestant youth groups in the Christian Endeavor movement of this great land. They did not fail to notice his reference to the support given India's missions from twelve nations besides the United States.

Here is a meeting-place of diversified Christian workers, speaking many languages, influenced by strong tides of custom and of attitude. The more remarkable, the more providential, that it is this difficult and complex field of mission work in which the Christian leadership can pool youth training and expression so successfully through Christian Endeavor's organization and program!

Yes, India gave us a challenge!

The Challenge from India

From an Address by

REV. VERE W. ABBEY

In representing Christian Endeavor work in the Union of India, Burma and Ceylon, I represent people who differ in costume, in language, in many ways. India has 220 languages. A student from India was strap-hanging in a New York subway car. A lady who noticed his difficulties moved over and made room for him to sit down.

"Thank you," said the student, "I am sorry to have cockroached upon you."

Said the lady, "You mean encroached."

He thought it over. "Thank you," he replied at last. "Now I understand. In speaking to a man you say 'cockroach,' but in speaking to a woman it is 'hencroach.'"

. . .

Christian Endeavor is world-wide in its challenge. In India we serve in missions with home roots in twelve nations besides the United States. India is not a country; it is a continent. People of the North differ from people of the South as much as do Scandinavians and Italians. But babies cry and people laugh in the same language everywhere. People are fundamentally one, especially in relation to God through Jesus. When you join a Christian Endeavor society you join hands with young people all over the world.

Unmatched Opportunities

We work in missions representing sixty denominations. Christian Endeavor is the one young people's society in India through which the Christian church can speak and act. We have the opportunity; the responsibilities are ours as well.

I think of the opportunity which lies before Christian Endeavor in the Orient. What shall we do about it? In Japan, as a result of the present situation, there is a great united church. The youth of the Christian community can work and speak through one or two denominations. Have we someone to organize the Christian youth of Japan, so that Christian Endeavor can be used of God in that country?

I know of no greater opportunity than in China today. We ought to have a dozen men ready to step into the work in China.

In the Philippines a great effort goes on to unite the youth of that country. Java is the only place in the world where there has been a mass movement away from Mohammedanism. We should be ready to step in and organize the young people there.

In India we boast of the union of Methodist youth with Christian Endeavor. (This brought 50,000 Methodist boys and girls into Christian Endeavor.) Our first task when we return to India will be a response to Bishop Azariah's request that we come to organize for union 180,000 Anglican young people.

There is a movement to unite all youth organizations in India—Y.M.C.A., Y.W.C.A., Christian Endeavor, and so forth.

We ought to have twenty men at once to go into the Orient.

There is no time to tell in detail of the work of Christian Endeavor in India. One great thing—carrying out the pledge, "I will seek to win others to Jesus Christ." Our most important committee is the committee on evangelism. In 1924 in Rangoon two of us missionaries sat down to lunch with Homer Rodeheaver and worked out a plan by means of which thousands were won for Christ.

Entering Forbidden Spots

A group of gospel teams working during the school holidays win hundreds in Burma. I visited one Scottish mission where there was a Christian Endeavor society of twenty members. I asked them, "What evangelistic work have you done?" "We're not preachers," they replied. "But you can do something," I said. They went to the pastor—it was the week for special evangelism. He said, "What do you want to do?" They named a destination—one of the states closed to preaching.

The pastor said, "You won't be allowed to preach there." They said, "We *can't* preach." They went into the closed area and stopped people on the street; they sold 75 to 80 Gospel portions to the people. They found there a back-slidden Christian who had married a Hindu and had been re-baptized a Hindu. They went to his home, and he came back to Christ. Months later, when they returned, they sold 500 copies of Gospel portions here. They found then that the high school principal and his assistant are Christians. That the superintendent of nurses in the hospital is a Christian. They couldn't build churches there, but the young people could tell the story of Christ in action, word, story and song, so that everywhere the young people wanted to come to Christ.

The Outcastes Organize

A great thing in India now is the mass movement of outcastes, sixty thousand of them. In India the castes are priest, soldier, merchant, artisan, and then there is the outcaste, an economic slave. Socially and spiritually also he is a slave, without hope. The outcastes have listened to the teaching of God's love and they come to Christ by the thousands. Illiterate, degraded, without hope, they accept Christ as fast as they understand. Then you have the difficulty of making a church out of them. The only way you can do this is to train them through Christian Endeavor, which is producing leadership for the church in India.

The president of the All-India Christian Endeavor Union was envied by his boss, and he was demoted from high school principal to principal of a middle school. Instead of complaining he set to work to raise the standards of the middle school and to raise money for a new building.

The former president of the union was paralyzed so that he couldn't walk. He regained the use of his body through sheer will power and the grace of God, and became a delegate to Madras.

A Boy Served Fifty Villages

About eight years ago I toured Assam. There are two missions—American Baptists and Welsh Continental Methodists. I spoke to the young people of the high school of the Welsh Mission and had a consecration service at the close of the meeting. A boy from the head-hunting Animist tribes, in school on a scholarship, gave his heart to Christ. He became a new Kizo. He was a senior but he couldn't pass in mathematics so he didn't graduate. He went home and taught in the village school, saved his money and returned to the seminary.

As an evangelist he worked in fifty villages, organized fifty-four Christian Endeavor societies with 5,227 members. One thousand young people were baptized and received into the church.

Two years ago, during the Golden Jubilee Christian Endeavor Convention in Calcutta, Kizo went sight-seeing. He had walked seven days and then rode four days on a train, by the way, to reach the Convention. Bitten by a mosquito he developed malarial fever. Thinking himself about to die he sent for the missionary. He explained that a few months before he had felt called to go to preach to a very wild tribe. He asked the police for a pass; it was refused because the people of that tribe had vowed to kill anyone who preached Christianity. Kizo said to himself, "I'll go without a pass," but when he reached the border he thought, "I'll lose my life if I go there," and turned back home.

"Pray for me," he urged the missionary, "that I do not die until I have made that visit."

Later the Convention in Assam wanted to make him president. He replied to their invitation, "I am going to preach to the forbidden tribe." His choice was between high honor and having his head cut off. Miraculously he was not killed. He has made two trips since then and has baptized seven families in that forbidden country.

These Speakers Called Us to Work

The speakers who have been quoted in this chapter represent some of the many reasons why the Rainbow Jubilee Convention will live for years in the memory of everyone who attended any considerable number of its thought-stirring, action-inviting sessions.

The "world reporters" called us to work. Showing us the need of men, picturing for us the sacrifices of other Christians who help to serve that need, they at once shamed young Americans for their complacency and warmed them for new vigor in the coming opportunities and responsibilities of Christ's advance.

Everything that had been promised for this Convention of a critical year had been fulfilled when the "world reporters" had given their messages to spellbound audiences. And yet there was more—much more—to make the anniversary Convention great and to warrant the many additional pages of this Convention record.

VI

Challenged in Our Own Land

American Religious Leaders Report

TWO of the familiar and best loved speakers in the Atlantic City Convention came to us from Hollywood.

The one, Dr. Louis H. Evans, formerly of Pittsburgh, but reared in California, has returned to his home state as the newly appointed pastor of First Presbyterian Church of Hollywood.

The other, Dr. Norman V. Peale of New York City, came from Hollywood to the Convention because he represented American Protestants in the "movie capital" while the famous story of "One Foot in Heaven" was cast into film and reeled into the familiar cans in which commercial pictures travel.

Dr. Peale was the closing speaker in the Friday evening session. Dr.

Bachrach

DR. LOUIS H. EVANS
Pastor, First Presbyterian Church of
Hollywood, California

DR. NORMAN V. PEALE
Pastor, Marble Collegiate Church,
New York City

Evans spoke in the closing session of the Convention, immediately before the final service of consecration that was led by President Poling.

Excerpts from the address of Dr. Norman Vincent Peale, pastor of the Marble Collegiate Church of New York City, begin with a reference to the important and unprecedented work that called him to Hollywood shortly before the Convention.

"One Foot in Heaven"

I have come to this Convention from a very great experience, one of the greatest experiences of my life. Last night at six o'clock I left Hollywood, and early Monday morning by means of the miracle of the airplane, I will be back on Warner Brothers' lot in California to resume my duties as technical adviser in the filming of the picture, "One Foot in Heaven."

Early last winter J. L. Warner, of Warner Brothers, wrote to Dr. Daniel A. Poling, Editor of *Christian Herald* and President of this great International Christian Endeavor movement, saying that they, the largest motion picture producers in the world, had decided to film Hartzell Spence's fascinating biography of his father. Mr. Warner said they wanted to bring to the screen the life of this admirable, rugged, and altogether lovable minister of the gospel, not only for the entertainment of the story but as representative of a class of men who had made a notable contribution to the upbuilding of this nation.

Mr. Warner requested Dr. Poling to aid Warner Brothers in securing a representative of the Protestant church to act as technical adviser in the production of the picture. The following committee was chosen: Bishop James Edward Freeman (Protestant Episcopal), Bishop Charles Wesley Flint (Methodist); Dr. Daniel A. Poling (Baptist), Editor of *Christian Herald*; Dr. F. H. Knubel (Lutheran); Dr. Edgar De Witt Jones (Christian).

I was given the honor of this appointment and arrived in Hollywood Monday, June 16, and will be there until early in August on this work.

You may be interested in my experience in Hollywood. One hour after arrival I was "on location" where the company was "shooting" a scene at the little old-fashioned San Gabriel railroad station which had been changed to "Laketon, Iowa," the first charge of the young minister and wife. This was the arrival scene, and it was intensely interesting to watch the old-fashioned, smoky train puff into this station, a place at which the train ordinarily does not stop.

Director and Stars Sympathetic

We met Irving Rapper, the director, a very capable young man who regards this picture as a great opportunity, both as to his own art and as a public service. We have found Mr. Rapper to have a very sensitive insight into the meaning of this story and he has a fine understanding of the character he is directing. The humorous elements in a minister's life will be shown always with respect and Mr. Rapper is also bringing out the greatness and power of this typical minister of the church. Under his direction the picture will have a message.

The part of the minister is taken by one of America's greatest screen actors, Fredric March. I like him tremendously. He is a man's man, a splendid personality, and this minister will certainly be no "sissy." Mr. March is the son of a Presbyterian elder of many years' standing. Father March was recently honored as the oldest director of the Y.M.C.A. in the state of Wisconsin. Fredric March told me he learned to act in Sunday school plays in Racine's First Presbyterian Church, plays written by his mother. Mr. March was eager to play this part and considers it a high point in his career. He fully enters into the spirit of the ministry and I told him recently he acts it so realistically that I am sure a Methodist bishop will appoint him to a church when this picture is completed. Fredric March as Rev. William Spence will be a notable character in American screen history.

Martha Scott, heroine of "Our Town" and "Cheers for Miss Bishop," is one of the greatest of the new stars of stage and screen. She is a young woman, class of 1932 at Michigan (that is all she has told me about her age). She is as sweet and lovely an American girl as I ever encountered. She has a truly great career before her and her part in this picture will add new laurels to the rapid development of a great American actress. Miss Scott personally is a very sweet and genuine person, totally unspoiled and sincere. The church people of the country may consider it good fortune indeed to have two stars of Christian heritage and religious background and of splendid personal character in the first important picture built around a minister.

The guiding mind and spirit in the filming of "One Foot in Heaven" is the producer, Robert Lord. In Hollywood, the producer is the high authority in the making of a picture and he bears the final responsibility. He is the general, or commanding officer, of the large number of people who work so efficiently together, each person doing his special task in an apparently intricate but marvelously efficient organization.

Mr. Lord is held in respect by all the employees, from the stars to the humblest workman. To them all he is "Bob" Lord, a familiarity always spoken with respect and genuine regard. He is democratic in all his contacts, with a friendly word for all, but I am told he is one of the best men in the business, with an intimate knowledge of this vast and complicated industry. A man of deep culture and splendid character, he is admirably suited to produce this first big moving picture of American church life.

Ten Things I Have Discovered About Hollywood

1. That a minister can feel very much at home in Hollywood.

2. That it is the hardest working place I ever saw.

3. That the people are not blase and sophisticated, but wholesome, friendly, home-loving folks.

4. That the handful of actors who have the bad reputations, the few irresponsibles, do not represent Hollywood and are frowned upon by the motion picture community.

5. That it is more than a money-making industry, for its leaders and personnel find a satisfaction in "getting over a message of Americanism and the better things."

6. That it is a vast, efficient place of business, where a great commodity is being produced for the pleasure of eighty million Americans, and not a scene of revelry.

7. That to watch the making of a movie is one of the most interesting and fascinating experiences any man can have. One marvels at the ingenuity and resourcefulness, the infinite patience and skill required. One's respect for the people who make the movies increases every day.

8. That Hollywood is on the way to learning that there is a high resourcefulness that need not "drag in" a drinking scene to fill up a dull spot in action.

9. That the public doesn't know Hollywood and should demand a more accurate account than is usually pictured. Hollywood needs a campaign to sell itself as it actually is to the country, for I believe the people are tired of doings of a few empty-headed glamour boys and girls who give the wrong impression of a great and decent industry. Hollywood would gain in public favor, and so in business and influence, if the country could be shown its real character.

10. That Hollywood is a mine for sermonic material and it will live in the sermons of this one parson in days to come.

Building a Man

It is a great thing when a man can thank God for a crisis because it gives him an opportunity to be a man. He is less than a man who fails to see in a difficult situation the opportunity to prove his faith in God and his courage. The greatest thing in the world is to make a man of yourself.

We lack faith in ourselves. Our tendency is to sit about and say, "Why don't THEY do it?"

We are told that the group is the repository of social unity—the mass. The mass never did consecrate itself; it has been the individual who stands apart from the mass who advances civilization. I wish I could talk to each one of you as an individual. I wish I could persuade you that the future of America doesn't depend on Congregationalists or Presbyterians but on you. What's wrong with your community? Don't wait for the mayor to change it. What's wrong with your church? Don't wait for the official board to act.

He Got Through the Mud

A young preacher in Iowa had as one of his churches a rural congregation in a district of very poor roads. His predecessor closed this church for three months every winter. On the first muddy Sunday this young man started out. Finally his car bogged down in the mud. He walked the last mile and found the church empty and cold. He built a fire. When he went to ring the bell he found that the rope was gone, so he climbed up and rang the bell with' his hands. After a while he saw a farmer running across the fields. Cried the farmer, "I've called them on the party line. They'll be here in half an hour." And so they were.

And the young minister preached with passion, and fervently the congregation sang "Faith of Our Fathers."

No, I'm not sorry for you young people. Times are hard but you are strong. March up against your difficulties and conquer them in the name of Jesus Christ. The majority of people who come to the psychological clinic in my church are under forty, many of them under thirty. You need peace in your hearts. How can you conquer fear and tension? You can bring your troubles to God. There is a therapeutic healing in His touch. Our country needs a revival of religion, for in this time of strain, people are being exposed to pressures of all kinds. We must bring them back to God so that with rational and cool minds they may attack the problems of the day. We must have a renewal of the grace of God to give peace and quietness to men's hearts.

If we can create a certain kind of persons in this hour we can save the world. You young people, touched with the splendor of God, can create in the Christian church a person who is magnificent, who carries no gun and has no bombs to drop, but who has something more powerful than any weapon ever invented.

Dr. Peale told of a Dutch skipper, separated from his family from whom no word came, who refused to bear hate and who told the New York clergyman that he prays for Hitler.

"I saw him grow," concluded the speaker, "until he became the symbol of the glory and majesty of Christians throughout the ages, those who rise above hate. If we can create people like him, we have the formula for the new world that is to come."

Crowd or Army?

Said Dr. Louis H. Evans, as he began his Sunday night address:
"I wonder if I am looking out at a crowd or an army. There's a war

on—a present fight against atheism, the liquor traffic, the amusement system, the divorce evil, the half-gods that men go about worshipping, unbelief entrenched in the hearts of men. For I am talking about spiritual warfare, in which we all have much at stake."

He continued:

Physical war is never final. Before Hitler was Napoleon. War won't change things. Unless we get to work as Christians to cut out the human cancer, the nations will rise again and again to knock each other out. Jesus Christ is the great Physician. We need Him to cleanse the bloodstream of the nations.

King Joash said Elisha was more of a protection to Israel than all the chariots and horses. God Almighty is our main refuge. Remember that when talking about physical defense!

There is a great army here. I don't know how many of you God can use. Gideon had 32,000 but by the time he got through with them there were but three hundred. You can't judge a convention by the size of its registration, but by the degree of its consecration. God tested Gideon's army on (1) attitude of heart, (2) equipment. Those who were afraid could go home. Twenty-two thousand went home. Are you afraid for yourself? Of the crowd, of laughter, ridicule, scorn? Of the Cross? If you are, you might as well go home like Gideon's men who feared what would happen next.

Is the church feeding itself on the Word of God to prepare itself for this struggle? Gideon's army, put to the test, did not have equipment for the fight. Only three hundred cupped their hands to drink quickly, remaining ready for action.

People don't want a religon that costs too much. Christianity hasn't a ghost of a chance to survive unless we give our hearts to Christ with greater fervor than youth give their hearts to Hitler and Stalin. By the practical tests, Gideon's army was whittled down to its three hundred. One to a hundred—that's about the way leaders come.

Al Capone said only three per cent of the population is criminal. If the good people stood together and were courageous enough they could run the Capones out of business.

Light for an Army

Gideon's army got its equipment. A light, a pitcher, a shout, a trumpet. We have a light; that's why we go to school and college. We have a spiritual light. Jesus gave light on four great problems. "What is God like?" was the first. He answered, "Ye that have seen me have seen the Father." Second, "What are we living for?" Third, "How is sin forgiven and set aside?" Fourth, "What about the future life?" The light is gone when Christ is gone.

The pitchers which held the lights of Gideon's men were earthenware, not silver or gold. You may be earthenware but give yourself just as you are—that is consecration. You'll get all you need to be worthy of your high purpose. Dwight L. Moody reached the third grade in school, but God used him to shake the world. The pitchers were breakable. Are you willing to be broken so the light of Christ can shine out? Some of us seem too crammed full of ourselves to have room for God's light.

The shout of Gideon's men terrified the enemy. They made so much noise that the enemy thought they were all captains. They'll think you've got something when you begin to shout about Jesus. The trumpet of victory? Blow a clear note for Jesus Christ, for no one can change life like He can. Jesus will win.

You know Hitler says, "I'm going to tear up the Christian church by the roots." But he cannot even find those roots. There is not a chance of Christianity's failure. The dictators are unwittingly becoming the gardeners of God, for there will be a great surge to Christianity following this war. "This is my Father's world, the battle is not done. Jesus who died shall be satisfied, and earth and heaven be one!"

While the World Changes

One more of the speakers who has earned a place on Christian Endeavor's platform on memorable occasions still to come is Dr. William Lloyd Imes, pastor of St. James Presbyterian Church of New York City. The powerful Negro leader and speaker framed his Sunday afternoon address so skillfully that the message was equally satisfying to the young delegates and to a number of older friends and ministers who were in the audience that day.

Some Changeless Values in a Changing World

From an Address by

DR. WILLIAM LLOYD IMES

It is my very great honor to greet you not only as one whose early Christian life was shaped and guided by the Christian Endeavor movement, but also especially as a representative of one man in every ten in this American nation—a man of African blood, and American to the very core.

My people have a rightful and serious stake in all that is dear to us in this country, and, by that same token, we are also world citizens and our blood and traditions span many continents and islands.

We have come from a slavery that degraded both man and master for over two centuries of unrequited toil in this new world. In spite of that we are not only citizens and friends today of all other racial groups in this land, but we are alive to the great currents of world thinking and action.

All over this new world, as well as the old, my people are winning their way, not by asking alms but opportunity. They too, with all of you, seek a better country, not only in the far-off divine event but in the present uptorn and heart-breaking world of evil which shakes an arrogant fist in the face of God and His righteousness.

Reason Shall Lead Us

One great pathway of our common faith in Christ is the simple but inevitable way of Reason. Not merely reasoning, or logic, but a deeper and stronger use of our utmost power of mind. We would have our very centers of thinking and planning dominated and directed by Him who is the Lord of the mind. This does not make us mere echoes of Christ. We think creatively, because His mind is in us. We think religiously, because we find in our religion that which compels us to follow Him in our processes of thought. He does not dishonor us by taking from us our God-given power of the intellect. Rather He inspires us to greater thoughts than otherwise we could attain—so that the adventure of living with Christ transcends race, creed, class, every condition.

Reality is another changeless value in this changing world, and now we do not mean merely the philosophical quest of that which is real as over against the imaginary, but a spiritual crusade in which the actual world, physical and spiritual alike, may be said to become the scene of God's redemptive work. Our religion is not afraid of reality. It dares to say "Let there be light!" It points unceasingly to the true Light. We challenge the so-called realism of foulness and filth and the literary output that is reminiscent of the barnyard. Well did that marvelous man of science, the late Charles Steinmetz, say of the struggle against false realism:

"The time will come when we will turn over our laboratories and libraries, our studies and our workshops into the practice of prayer and the search for God; and we shall make more progress then than in any previous generation."

How exciting and exhilarating to find that the more we learn of the starry heavens above, the more we know of the moral law within!

Righteousness for America

Righteousness is the crowning value of this changing world. Our forms of thought change and our modes of science and skill in the arts vary, but ever there is a single divine truth which keeps our course clear. Matthew Arnold once said: "Nothing will do except righteousness, and no other version of righteousness will do except that of Christ."

The Christian accepts the challenge. He says Christ has the version of righteousness which is supreme. And then he does something about that belief. He puts it into the arena of life. He adventures with Christ in new and difficult places.

If he is a black man in America, he struggles to gain respect for his fellows who are asked to fight for democracy but are denied the right to work in defense industries. If he is in India, he says that God's order is not one of upholding an old order of imperialism on one hand or caste on the other, but an order of brotherhood and fellowship, and only in Christ can men gain that fully. Go where you will, this international spirit of the free man in Christ is taking possession of our world. Do not be distracted by the utter crassness and brutality of this present military conflict. It is a terrible and fearful present fact, but the real struggle lies deeper. Man is God's child, not made for the sport of time and chance nor for the ruthless exploitation by his fellows. Any system built upon evil and greed must fail. Here is our ultimate battle. Righteousness exalteth a nation, but sin is a reproach to any people.

Christians Must Unite

Three hours before the Convention Parade was to break precedent by forming and marching on the famous Boardwalk, a friend of youth and of Christian Endeavor from the leadership of the United Church of Canada was speaking on the other demonstrations youth can make of its inter-faith unity, its ecumenicity.

Dr. Manson Doyle, associate secretary of the Board of Christian Education of the United Church of Canada, chose for his subject "What Christian Youth Faces in the Ecumenical Church."

He said in part:

There must be a very large percentage of Christian youth whose understanding of the church is limited to their own denominational institutions. They simply have not seen the necessity for investigating church life, faith, and procedure beyond the bounds of their own personal experience. They probably regard their own ways as better than those of others, but they seem to take for granted that however faulty other churches may be in details differing from their own traditions, these churches have a central faith in Christ and a moral authority and practice soundly Christian and worthy of esteem.

We find youth almost always generous and liberal in their expressed judgments of other communions. Even when they find it necessary to criticize, the criticism is invariably without animus. Even among groups of young people quite uninformed as to the history and the doctrine of the churches they know, there is a tacit recognition of some essential features of Christian faith which makes them worthy to be classed as truly belonging to the mystic body of Christ.

There have been held during the last few years and within the lifetime of all of those but the very youngest present, a series of great and important conferences. It would rather seem that each of these conferences—Jerusalem, Edinburgh, Oxford, Madras, Amsterdam, and all the others—had been called under the pressure of some definite need which, in part at least, it seems to have met. Then the succeeding conferences came logically and psychologically in sequence to the conference already held. It is significant for us today that the very last of these councils, completed on the very sunset day of world peace, scarcely dispersed before the war clouds burst, was the first World Conference of Christian Youth.

The Christian Youth Conference refused to issue any official findings. It followed a policy of a previous semi-world-conference of the Student Christian Federation, to discuss and study the great question of the varieties of Christian faith and to leave entirely to the participating individuals and groups the formulating and stating of such findings as could be arrived at. It is necessary to quote from the findings of groups who, at the Conference or on their return, put down definitely their conclusions as to the outcome.

Some Christians Want No Church

There is a section of very earnest youth who would make no deliberate attempt at organizing an established, visible church. They ask only for liberty of group action and expression, with freedom to put their convictions into speech and action, and their hope seems to be that the intrinsic power of their ideas will be all that is necessary to save the world.

Still another group despairs of the church. They charge her with lack of courage, with bondage to tradition, with the weakness of submitting to the control of self-interested individuals, and so they would demand the organization of a new order within the church.

A third and really important group is made up of young people who have belonged to the church or at least have early associations with the Sunday school and the young people's society, and generally have a strong Christian family tradition—but whose active participation in the serious affairs of life has been dedicated to some special movement or organization outside the church. Usually such movements are engaged in one phase of the work which the church stands for, but these young people have evidently lost hope of the church making progress in these special lines. They have in my judgment made the mistake of putting all their active Christian convictions into the work of a movement or organization which gives all of its time and energy to one phase of the Christian program. Though they may be in attendance occasionally at church, they give their real thinking and real service to outside institutions.

There is a fourth group, very decidedly loyal to the Christian church, and usually among the front-line leadership of Christian youth in their community. But they will have nothing to do with "meantime measures" for this ecumenical effort. They demand corporate union of churches at once. They are unwilling to give time and effort to those movements within the church which are an evidence of cooperative good will though they do not go the length of advocating corporate union.

One Great Group to Be Won

Of course there is that great group of youth whose childhood was lived in a Christian background but who have been captivated by the general hurry and interest of secular life. These are people who might, during the next two or three months, be brought into full commitment to Jesus Christ and His cause, and become a most intelligent and effective group in ecumenical Christianity.

But all of these groups, and others, are dependent for the positive leadership which will eventually bring about a world order, upon the faithfulness, intelligence, and earnest effort of the great company of Christian youth who believe that if the church will courageously face the wrongs within and before her, she will by God's guidance and grace be able to move the world—as she has done again and again in times gone by, into those channels which are in accordance with the mind and program of Jesus Christ.

We have no doubt that you represent hundreds of thousands of such youth who stand ready to do their part.

It should be remembered that no generation of youth suddenly takes over from its predecessors. Youth is slowly assimilated into the ranks of experienced leadership and that slow process begins when youth is willing in some small and almost undesirable way to count actively in the building of the Kingdom of God. One generation does not stop and another take over; they dovetail into each other. Youth is under the necessity today, as never before, of picking out the great things, at the very center of which lies this idea of an ecumenical church, a great invisible host whose hearts are already aflame with a living faith in Christ, who may not know each other by name but who nevertheless in that mystic fellowship of believing souls are strengthened by each other's very existence.

Thanks to the foreign missionary movement of our fathers' generation, the church today is the one institution which is rooted in the soil of many countries and includes the most divine groups of men within its fellowship. This is a fact of great encouragement. It means a supra-national, supra-racial community of men and women who find inspiration in the same Scripture, worship the same God revealed in Christ, and stand committed to the revelation of a divine Kingdom—who, in other words, are the great body of living members in the ecumenical church.

A Sturdy and Valued Layman Speaks

For a number of years, Hon. Frederick A. Wallis has raised a mighty and prophetic voice in many Christian Endeavor conventions. A former president of the New York State Christian Endeavor Union, now residing in Kentucky, his career has included service as Commissioner of Correction of the City of New York and United States Commissioner of Immigration at Ellis Island in New York harbor.

"The gates at Ellis Island should swing in both directions," he told the delegates in the Friday morning session. He spoke on—

What Christian Youth Faces in America

The gates should swing inward in kind and cordial hospitality to the good and worthy immigrants, those persons who are in sympathy with American ideals and are willing to work and become naturalized and a corporate part of the United States.

But those same gates should swing outward, to make America eternally impassable to men and women who by word or deed would threaten the peace and tranquillity of this American nation or who in any way attempt to pull down the pillars of Americanism.

The United States has often been described as the Melting Pot of the Nations. Some of us do not realize the accuracy of the description, but a study of statistics shows what a mixture we really are in races and nations and religions.

That this hodgepodge of races and faiths can learn, as we are learning, to live together in peace and amity demonstrates the fact that world peace is not an impossible dream. It requires living according to the principles of tolerance and goodwill. This is one of the things that America can give the world—this final denial of stupid racial theories which would divide the world into little blood-tight compartments of inbred racial groups. The soil of a common country, the tie of a common language, the link of a common ideal of freedom—these form the ground on which civilized men may stand together and march together.

The Holy Communion Service

Sunday Morning, July 13, 8:00 A.M.

"THIS DO IN REMEMBRANCE OF ME"

PRELUDE

HYMN—"When Morning Gilds the Skies"

INVOCATION AND LORD'S PRAYER

RESPONSIVE LESSON—Psalm 103

PRAYER

HYMN—"Beneath the Cross of Jesus"

THE LORD'S SUPPER

The Words of Institution

Prayer of Institution (unison)

Most gracious God, the Father of our Lord Jesus Christ, whose once offering up of Himself upon the cross we commemorate before Thee, we earnestly desire Thy fatherly goodness to accept this our sacrifice of praise and thanksgiving.

And we pray Thee to bless and sanctify with Thy Word and Spirit these Thine own gifts of Bread and Wine which we set before Thee, that we may receive by faith Christ crucified for us, and so feed upon Him that He may be made one with us and we with Him.

And here we offer and present unto Thee ourselves, our souls and bodies, to be a reasonable, holy and living sacrifice unto Thee, praying that all we who are partakers of this Holy Communion may find that in this place Thou givest peace;

Through Jesus Christ our Lord, to whom, with Thee and the Holy Spirit, be the glory and the praise, both now and evermore. Amen.

The Administering of the Bread

The Administering of the Cup

Prayer of Thanksgiving and Consecration (unison)

Almighty God, our Heavenly Father, we thank Thee for this holy hour. Thou hast brought us to Thy banqueting house and Thy banner over us is love We have been refreshed in spirit by the presence of Thy Son, our living Lord, whose victorious death we have commemorated. We have come from all the corners of our nation and from many churches and homes, but we are all one in Him. We thank Thee for our precious fellowship in Him and with each other. As we go upon our way we would consecrate ourselves anew to the service of our fellow men in Jesus' name. We would go forth under the sign of His Cross to fight the good fight of faith and to endure to the end.

May Thy kingdom of righteousness, goodwill and peace come among all men. May all injustice and evil be overthrown. Send us forth in the power of Thy Holy Spirit to do even "greater things than these" according to our Master's promise, who first chose us, and whom we have chosen in loving obedience. And to Thee, Father, Son, and Holy Ghost, one God, will we ascribe everlasting praise, world without end. Amen.

HYMN—"O Jesus, I Have Promised"

BENEDICTION AND MIZPAH (unison)

VII

A Worshipping Convention

"Keep the splendor of God in the souls of men."--
Dr. Oscar F. Blackwelder, in a Quiet Hour Talk

IT was not surprising, yet it was cause for rejoicing, that the primary place in the Convention program and in the attention of the delegates was given to worship.

The Daily Quiet Hour was observed by all. Promptly and reverently the delegates came by the thousands to this early service, at which searching thoughts for the day were expressed by Dr. Sockman and Dr. Blackwelder.

Here thoughts were planted for many days to come. It was good to be together in these well planned meetings when the day was still new and the delegates and leaders turned quietly to God in prayer.

Each assembling of the Convention delegates had an appropriate and natural emphasis on worship. So begun, each meeting of day and night was full of power and leading.

And at the close of each evening session, when a full day of activities had been the lot of every delegate, the young people went quickly and gladly to the worship services of the state delegations. That is in the great tradition of Christian Endeavor conventions—and the second sixty years of the movement have begun with this tradition honored and strengthened by the inspiring worship gatherings of Atlantic City 1941.

Illinois delegates were among those who met for worship on the beach, where the waves played an obligato to their hymns. Pennsylvania's delegates were so numerous that the late evening worship service overflowed the largest assembly hall of the hotel in which most of their number stayed.

As is invariably true, the Holy Communion Service on Sunday morning was for many Endeavorers the most sacred and memorable part of the Atlantic City Convention. Dr. William Hiram Foulkes was prevented by ill health from being present in person, yet the gracious remembrance of his presence and leadership at other similar services and the conviction of his presence in thought and in prayer were very real.

Dr. A. E. Cory, trustee of the International Society of Christian Endeavor, presided, assisted by Dr. W. A. MacTaggart of Canada and a large group of ministers and laymen under the chairmanship of Rev. W. W. Payne of Atlantic City.

Four Mornings in Quiet Hour Worship

Dr. Ralph W. Sockman, minister of Christ Methodist Church of New York City, was Quiet Hour speaker for Wednesday and Thursday mornings.

On the following two days, the Quiet Hour message was given by Dr. Oscar F. Blackwelder, minister of the Lutheran Church of the Reformation, Washington, D. C.

The first quarter-hour of each of these refreshing services, from 8:30 to 8:45, was devoted to the singing of hymns, and at no period in the Convention were delegates more tuneful and inspired in song. Each such service concluded at 9:15, in time for the Educational Conferences which began ten minutes later in the commodious Convention Auditorium's many rooms and halls and elsewhere.

From Dr. Sockman's Talks

One of the most effective sermons ever given was preached by Peter, who said, "Ye killed the Prince of Life." In his translation of the New Testament, Moffatt writes, "Ye have killed the Pioneer of Life."

These translations seem to suggest different aspects of life. "Prince" suggests royal ancestry, rich background, but "pioneer" suggests modest ancestry, no background— yet both are applied to our Lord.

Truly He was regal. "He spoke as one having authority." He said, "Ye call me Master and Lord, and ye say well; for so I am." Yet He was also a pioneer. He started something so new, so significant, that we date our calendars from His birth.

"Prince" suggests background. "Pioneer" suggests foreground. Some people see nothing good but what is old. They are the reactionaries. Some are impatient with the past and run after every new idea. They are the radicals. Jesus would not have us take either view. He might want us to have something like a driving mirror in which you see the road behind while keeping your major vision on the road ahead. Collision can come from behind, especially when we turn left. (In our speech, "left" is the turn toward that which is new!) In architecture you cannot create new forms until you know the old. Religion should think of the early church climbing out of the catacombs, extending to Europe, girdling the globe. We need background. Jesus takes us all the way to Gabriel.

But we must not look backward only. We could end wars, injustice, want, if Christians could remember the ideals of their youth. Alas, they become "practical"! Man reaches the peak of his physical strength sometime in the forties, his mental strength in the fifties, his spiritual peak never, so long as he sees the world climbing upward. You get that point of view best when you get background. You must keep background and foreground together.

"Prince" suggests organization, "pioneer" the lonely individual efforts. We need a better adjustment of both. We need organization. In a one-room school the cry, "Fire!" is enough to get the pupils to safety. In a large school the cry causes panic and death. It is unsafe to live in a high-powered world without organization. We recognize that in industry; why not in religion?

Why? Some say, "Because I can keep closer to God by myself." No doubt I could feel close to God some morning on this lovely shore, but I couldn't keep up that feeling or pass it on to my children unless there was organization. Worship is like a ship in a canal. The sluice gates close behind the ship and open before it, and the ship sails off to a higher level. This Quiet Hour is supposed to do something like that. When we come together we get the lift of God. Yes, we need the church.

DR. RALPH W. SOCKMAN
Pastor, Christ Methodist Church,
New York City

DR. OSCAR F. BLACKWELDER
Pastor, Church of the Reformation,
Washington, D. C.

But sometimes organization takes the place of individual effort. We organize everything. William Allen White once said that if three Americans fell from an airplane, before they reached the ground they would be organized as president, vice-president, and secretary. Organization cannot do the work without individual effort. The course in medical school is so hard that some students drop out each year, but those who stick find that all the lectures have point when laboratory work begins. Young people drop out of the church when we fail to take them over from the lecture-room to the laboratory.

Jesus stopped the disciples halfway through their course. At Caesarea Philippi, He asked them, "Whom say men that I am?" They gave the current answers, but Jesus persisted. "But whom say YE that I am?" and then Peter answered, "Thou art the Christ, the Son of the living God."

When we think of "prince" we think of "power over." When we think of "pioneer" we think of "power for." So much literature trains you to have power over others. Jesus says that he who is greatest is he who serves. You can get power over, as Japan over China, and Germany over Europe, but that kind of power is short-lived. Jesus says, "I am among you as one who serves." Jesus will outlive the dictators, for His is the "power for" others.

Dr. Mather in his "Religious Beliefs" writes, "I believe that there is a divine administration over the universe, guaranteeing the triumph of personal and spiritual values." A questioner asked, "How can you believe that when Jesus was defeated?" Dr. Mather answered in turn, "In the light of what He did, what has been done in His name since, do you believe that He was defeated?" I don't!

From Dr. Blackwelder's Talks

The purpose of this Quiet Hour, as I see it, is that each one of us may come to a fresh and more intelligent commitment to Christ and that we may strengthen a few convictions that are essential to the sacredness of human life.

It is said that the gloomy philosopher, Schopenhauer, who was extremely odd in appearance, was taking a walk one morning. A stranger approached him and asked, "Tell me, who in the name of fate are you?" Replied Schopenhauer, "Ah, that I only knew!" It is the province of the church to tell us what we are.

Twenty-five to fifty years ago, man exaggerated his powers. Swinburne, the cynical poet, wrote, "Glory to man in the highest, for man is the master of things." We now call such talk drivel. Over-confidence has led to a lack of confidence. During the last two decades, man has been described by the psychologist, analyzed by the physical scientist, but not interpreted. The question remains, "What is a man worth after all?"

The philosopher makes a man at home in the universe, the historian makes him the heir of the ages, but something more is needed to make a man a good neighbor. Religion must do that.

A man is more than anything to which he belongs—class or race or nation. When you think of a man as rich or poor, you make him an adjective to modify an economic system. When you think of him as white or black, you make him an adjective to modify a race. The only relationship in which man can be regarded as more than an adjective is that of man's relationship to his Creator. How sacred is human life? You are as sacred as God who made you. We are made in His own image. Apply one commandment to that—"Thou shalt not take the name of the Lord thy God in vain." God's name stands for Him. "Thou shalt not take the image of the Lord thy God in vain." Man stands for God.

We are not fully controlled by our glands, our heredity, our environment. We are affected also by our purposes, our plans, our ideals.

We are not just pushed by our past and pulled by our future, for we are the children of God. We are sacred. We dare not violate the person of our mind and body, or that of any other person.

How sacred is human life? Whitehead said, "Man deserves to be visited by Him who has ordained the stars." The Christian faith is that man has been so visited. The Incarnation means that God was in Jesus. It means also that He is in every one of us. "The spirit of man is the temple of the Lord." You see God pass by in the poems of Tennyson, the plays of Shakespeare, the paintings of Raphael, the sculpture of Michelangelo. You see God pass by in the person of the humblest man or woman you meet on the Boardwalk.

"Do not think more highly of yourself than you ought to think"—but be sure to think highly enough! Over-humility is as bad as over-pride. The Scotchman's prayer, "Lord, help me to have a high opinion of myself," is sometimes a good one.

There are two points I want to draw out of the Christian doctrine of man: the first, a sense of responsibility to man dependent upon accountability to God; the second, a sense of balance.

William Mather Lewis said that he would like to have written over the entrance to every institution of learning, "A balanced life in an unbalanced world." How can you get that sense of balance? Through a sense of direction. Through the proper proportion of work, play, love, and worship. The sense of balance comes out of the Christian doctrine of man. May man's value be a renewed conviction in our minds this morning.

Remember the inscription on the tomb of Dwight L. Moody in Northfield, "He that doeth the will of God abideth forever."

Dr. Blackwelder closed this talk with an unusually meaningful brief prayer, which included these words: "If error has been spoken, may the Spirit of Truth erase it from our memories."

Convention Worship Services

Two of the impressive and thoroughly prepared worship services of the Convention are quoted in full, to complete this brief review of how the Rainbow Jubilee Convention delegates met together in public praise and confession and consecration in those sunlit days along the shore.

SERVICE OF WORSHIP FOR THURSDAY, JULY 10

"The Commanding Position of Jesus Christ"

The Leader: A Call to Worship.

> For unto us a child is born, unto us a son is given: and the government shall be upon his shoulder: and his name shall be called Wonderful, Counselor, the mighty God, the everlasting Father, the Prince of Peace. Of the increase of his government and peace there shall be no end, upon the throne of David, and upon his kingdom, to order it, and to establish it with judgment and justice from henceforth even for ever. The zeal of the Lord of hosts will perform this.—(Isa. 9:6, 7.)

A Hymn of Exaltation to Christ: "Crown Him with Many Crowns," first stanza.

> Crown him with many crowns,
> The Lamb upon his throne;
> Hark! how the heavenly anthem drowns
> All music but its own!
> Awake, my soul, and sing
> Of him who died for thee,
> And hail him as thy matchless King
> Through all eternity.

The Leader: These shall make war with the Lamb, and the Lamb shall overcome them: for he is Lord of lords, and King of kings: and they that are with him are called, and chosen, and faithful.—(Rev. 17:14.)

The Hymn: The second stanza of the same hymn.

> Crown him the Son of God
> Before the world began,
> And ye, who tread where he hath trod,
> Crown him the Son of man,
> Who every grief hath known
> That wrings the human breast,
> And takes and bears them for his own,
> That all in him may rest.

The Leader: He that hath my commandments, and keepeth them, he it is that loveth me: and he that loveth me shall be loved of my Father, and I will love him, and will manifest myself to him.—(John 14:21.)

The Hymn: The third stanza of the same hymn.

> Crown him the Lord of Life
> Who triumphed o'er the grave,
> And rose victorious in the strife
> For those he came to save.
> His glories now we sing
> Who died, and rose on high,
> Who died, eternal life to bring,
> And lives that death may die.

The Leader: Peace I leave with you, my peace I give unto you: not as the world giveth, give I unto you. Let not your heart be troubled, neither let it be afraid.—(John 14:27.)

The Hymn: The fourth stanza of the same hymn.

> Crown him the Lord of peace,
> Whose power a sceptre sways
> From pole to pole, that wars may cease,
> And all be prayer and praise!
> Crown him with many crowns
> As thrones before him fall,
> Crown him, ye kings, with many crowns
> For he is King of all.

Unison Devotional Reading (all reading in concert):

> O thou great Friend to all the sons of men,
> Who once appeared in humblest guise below,
> Sin to rebuke, to break the captive's chain,
> And call thy brethren forth from want and woe.
>
> We look to thee: thy truth is still the light
> Which guides the nations, groping on their way,
> Stumbling and falling in disastrous night,
> Yet hoping ever for the perfect day.
>
> Yes, thou art still the life; thou art the way
> The holiest know—light, life, and way of heaven;
> And they who dearest hope and deepest pray
> Toil by the light, life, way which thou has given.
> *(Theodore Parker)*

Unison Prayer: The Lord's Prayer.

A Hymn of Appreciation to Christ: "Hail, Thou Once Despised Jesus."

> Hail, thou once despised Jesus,
> Hail, thou Galilean King!
> Thou didst suffer to release us,
> Thou didst free salvation bring.
> Hail, thou agonizing Saviour,
> Bearer of our sin and shame!
> By thy merit we find favor,
> Life is given through thy name.
>
> Paschal Lamb, by God appointed,
> All our sins on thee were laid;
> By almighty love anointed,
> Thou has full atonement made.
> All thy people are forgiven,
> Through the virtue of thy blood;
> Opened is the gate of heaven,
> Peace is made 'twixt man and God.

SERVICE OF WORSHIP FOR SUNDAY MORNING,

JULY 13

"The Worship of God"

Responsive Call to Worship (all standing).

Leader: The Lord reigneth; let the people tremble: He sitteth between the cherubims; let the earth be moved.

The People: The Lord is great in Zion; and he is high above all people.

Leader: The king's strength also loveth judgment; thou dost establish equity, thou executest judgment and righteousness in Jacob.

The People: Exalt ye the Lord our God, and worship at his footstool; for he is holy.

Hymn of Praise: "The Doxology" (all standing).

The Reading of God's Word: Psalm 93 (by the leader).

A Hymn of Praise: "Holy, Holy, Holy."

> Holy, holy, holy! Lord God Almighty!
> Early in the morning our song shall rise to thee:
> Holy, holy, holy! merciful and mighty!
> God in three persons, blessed Trinity!
>
> Holy, holy, holy! all the saints adore thee,
> Casting down their golden crowns around the glassy sea;
> Cherubim and seraphim falling down before thee,
> Who wert, and art, and evermore shalt be.
>
> Holy, holy, holy! though the darkness hide thee,
> Though the eye of sinful man thy glory may not see,
> Only thou art holy; there is none beside thee,
> Perfect in power, in love, and purity.
>
> Holy, holy, holy! Lord God Almighty!
> All thy works shall praise thy name, in earth, and sky, and sea;
> Holy, holy, holy! merciful and mighty!
> God in three persons, blessed Trinity!

The Reading of God's Word: Psalm 103:1-14 (by a reader).

Special Music.

Worship Pathways to God (while the organ plays quietly).

First Reader: "Give us grace, O God, to listen to thy call, to obey thy voice, and to follow thy guiding. Thou leadest us to pleasures that never fade, to riches which no moth nor rust can corrupt or destroy. Unsearchable riches are in thy hand. O give us grace to know the value of them, and to covet them. Thou leadest us to fountains of living water; suffer us not to wander or turn aside till we attain unto the pleasures which are at thy right hand for evermore. Establish, settle, strengthen us, that our goodness may not be like the early dew, which passeth away; but make us steadfast, immovable, always abounding in the work of the Lord, forasmuch as we know that our labor is not in vain in the Lord. Grant this, we beseech thee, for thy dear Son, Jesus Christ's sake." Amen.

Second Reader: By prayer we come to God.

> Prayer is the soul's sincere desire
> Unuttered or expressed;
> The motion of a hidden fire
> That trembles in the breast.
>
> (*James Montgomery*)

Third Reader: By the Holy Scriptures we come to God. "The Bible is one of the greatest blessings bestowed by God upon the children of men. It has God for its author, salvation for its end, and truth without any mixture for its matter. It is all pure, all sincere; nothing too much, nothing wanting." (*Locke*)

Fourth Reader: By the orderliness, majesty, mystery, beauty, and grandeur of God's world we come to him.

> Thou art, O God, the life and light
> Of all this wondrous world we see;
> Its glow by day, its smile by night,
> Are but reflections caught from thee.
> Where'er we turn thy glories shine,
> And all things fair and bright are thine.
>
> (*Thomas Moore*)

Fifth Reader: By the example and experience of great souls we come to God.

> A noble army, men and boys,
> The matron and the maid,
> Around the Saviour's throne rejoice,
> In robes of light arrayed:
> They climbed the steep ascent of heaven
> Through peril, toil, and pain:
> O God, to us may grace be given
> To follow in their train.
>
> (*Reginald Heber*)

Sixth Reader: By faith in Jesus Christ we come to God.

> God, it may be, has other words for other worlds,
> But for our world the word of God is Christ.

Hymn: "Our God, Our Help in Ages Past."

Worship in Tithes and Offerings.

Special Music.

The Sermon.

Closing Hymn.

Benediction.

International

Officers

Head the

Parade

The British

Empire Was

Represented

The

Massachusetts

Delegation

VIII

Parade and Pageant

IT is very exceptional for Atlantic City's government to permit a parade upon the Boardwalk.

To the thousands of summer vacationists who crowded hotel verandas and sun decks and lined the Boardwalk, this parade was a striking suggestion of the power of the world-wide youth movement which is Christian Endeavor.

Singing the hymns of the church and with banners and floats declaring for peace and pledging allegiance to Christ, more than six thousand young people followed Dr. Poling and the officers of the International Society of Christian Endeavor at a brisk and hearty pace.

With Dr. Poling marched his attractive daughters, Billie and Jane. Homer Rodeheaver, another "front-liner," was greeted by many admirers along the way. Mrs. Poling in an "official" and precedent-breaking automobile won hearty applause all along the Boardwalk.

Dr. W. A. MacTaggart, in a response to the address of welcome at the first Convention session, had said, "Christian Endeavor will keep marching."

And how these hosts of Endeavoring youth marched!

Utah Earned Top Ranking

The delegates from Utah were first in line, because their union attained the highest percentage of quotas of registrations for the Convention. Georgia youth followed, wearing choir gowns and carrying a banner with the words which were to appear so often in parade floats and banners, "Always—For Christ and the Church." A beautifully decorated float showed a fine selection of "Georgia peaches"!

A small but vigorous delegation from the distant State of Washington came next in line. Albert Arend of Washington was head of the First Division of the parade.

Florida's delegates followed a cross. They included young persons dressed as Seminole Indians, a large representation from St. Petersburg, and marchers doing the much practiced F-L-O-R-I-D-A step.

Each member of Tennessee's marching force carried one of the letters which spelled out "Christian Endeavor."

The District of Columbia delegation bore proudly the famous basket of flowers presented to Pauline Shoemaker, the new Associate President of the International Society, whose election on the preceding night was

PRE-CONVENTION REGISTRATION CAMPAIGN

When the count was made in the registration campaign conducted in advance of the Convention the following states were found to be in the lead Each received a properly numbered banner as an award, and was assigned the corresponding position in the great Boardwalk Parade The rankings were made on the basis of the percentage each state attained of its assigned quota of registrations

1.	Utah	156%	6	District of Columbia	
2	Georgia	132%	7	Kentucky	
3	Washington	106%	8	California	
4	Florida		9	Vermont	
5	Tennessee		10	Maryland	

In the contest for the most beautiful and effective float in the Convention Parade the following were the awards

First Place   Maryland   Second Place   Georgia

still being celebrated. "D. C." girls were charming in blue and white sailor dresses with white stars. The boys wore red and white hats.

The Golden Rule Union of Washington, D. C., was resplendent in blue and red satin capes. A superb living representation of the Statue of Liberty was the much applauded feature of this delegation.

Dapper Colonels, Lovely Belles

Kentucky colonels in spotless white suits, broad-brimmed hats and snowy goatees bowed and inquired pleasantly, "How ah yo' all?" With them were Kentucky belles, lovely in their long, flowered-chintz gowns. The girls curtsied demurely as they passed the reviewing line of International Society officers, for those front-line paraders had fallen out to exchange greetings with the state delegations that marched by.

California's parade delegation carried gay parasols of blue and yellow and bore striking banners.

Then came Maryland's Endeavorers, proclaiming theirs "the first state to allow religious freedom." Yellow-banded high hats and yellow boleros over white dresses and suits made an effective appearance. The state flag and the American flag were carried with dignity. A float showed scenes of "Christian Endeavor around the World." State officers rode in a decorated automobile. Balloons bobbed merrily along with the marchers who followed the car.

Indiana helped us to remember again that this was the Rainbow Jubilee observance. Their "bow of promise" was glorious and well executed.

Eyes on the Next Convention

In the parade, as on many other occasions, Colorado's fine delegation invited the International Society and all its friends to meet in Denver for the North American Convention of 1943.

Becoming and smart were Michigan's capes and the fine representatives who wore them.

"Yippee!" Who could that be? Surely it was Texas, with its young people doffing sombreros and brandishing toy guns.

Delaware delegates each carried a large fluffy yellow chick—cut from cardboard and mounted on a stick. The leaders bore a huge blue chicken. Their banner proclaimed them true Endeavorers, "For Christ and the Church."

The Long March Continued

New Hampshire girls were pretty in white dresses decorated with red clovers. Her boys wore white suits.

Wisconsin's theme was Indians. "Tall corn" and "wild roses" were emblems for Iowa's marchers. Virginia brought a message of Christian Endeavor activity "down where the South begins."

West Virginians carried bright balloons. Their costumes were particularly effective; the girls wore red and white blouses, white skirts, red socks, and straw hats, while the boys' shirts were yellow.

A whole parade in itself was the mighty delegation from Pennsylvania. The very young George Klauder, looking sturdy and manly in long white trousers, led the delegation. A band gaily costumed followed this drum major, and the procession of the white-clad Keystone State Endeavorers, topped with tall red hats, seemed unending.

Marching especially to honor President Poling was a large delegation from this leader's church, the Baptist Temple in Philadelphia.

Schuylkill Branch of the Philadelphia Union threw into the crowd many candies wrapped with this message, "It's sweet to belong to C. E."

The Pilgrim Fathers and Mothers of Massachusetts were ably portrayed by the delegates in capes and tall-crowned hats. And bells tinkled as the Bay State brethren marched.

The Host State Well Represented

New Jersey's usual orange and black appeared this time fashioned into bonnets with long streamers. Fifty-nine "Long-timers" marched, proudly conscious of New Jersey's Christian Endeavor history. Cumberland and Salem Counties presented a most attractive float, as did also Atlantic County. Other New Jersey units, with large delegations of marchers, showed that the movement flourishes in the state that played host to this notable Convention.

"Bell hops" hailed from Illinois—a goodly number of them. The costume was fashed from blue cloth splattered with white dots. Missouri had a synthetic mule in line, and this feature called for laughs and shouts all along the march. New York marched in vivid red and white capes. Maine's delegates with pardonable pride proclaimed theirs the birth state of Christian Endeavor. Connecticut, Ohio, Rhode Island,

and Canada were represented in the big procession.

Many parades offer more gorgeous costumes, more bands in proportion to marchers, more precision in marching order. But this parade was impressive, not because of elaborate and expensive displays or painful hours of rehearsal. It impressed Atlantic City's people and her guests and the Conventioneers themselves, because there was a light in the eyes of the boys and girls and older friends who marched—a light that gave its message of sincerity and devotion.

That parade was one promise of a better world—a world in which constructive goodwill shall reign in the spirit of the living Christ.

Telling Christian Endeavor's Story

The many and interesting notes made by the Recorder of this Convention, both at Atlantic City and immediately afterward, dealt only fleetingly with one of the most impressive and pleasurable events connected with the Rainbow Jubilee Convention program.

This omission is understandable, for it is the Recorder of these daily activities of six thousand youth at Atlantic City who wrote and directed the pageant she did *not* report for us. The Editor takes responsibility, and gladly, for the comments that follow.

Saturday's pageant was designed to be the outstanding feature of one of the most popular evenings of the whole Convention. It would follow the parade, always colorful and dramatic in the long and honored line of International Christian Endeavor Conventions. It would precede by not many hours the beginning of the Sunday program in the impressive All-Convention Communion Service, and with services of worship and inspiration filling all the remainder of that glorious closing day. Such an event must have high qualities in composition, color, music, dramatic episodes, cast, and direction, to live up to the expectations and the possibilities.

Catherine Miller Balm's Rainbow Jubilee Pageant had these qualities, and in abundance. It was a striking event, with many breath-taking moments, in the midst of a Convention that made history in every hour of its life.

The story it told was familiar to many who saw and heard the episodes on the Assembly Hall stage. These found new meaning in the events recounted and a more vivid appreciation of the sheer drama of Christian Endeavor's growth and service for sixty years.

The story was sparklingly new to many others who enjoyed this pageant. These carry with them forever an appreciation of Christian Endeavor's pioneers, its heroes, its fellowship of quiet and even anonymous serving members around the world. No history printed to be read could tell their story so well.

Thank you, Catherine Balm, for producing this story that we all wanted to know better!

The Rainbow Jubilee Pageant
"FOR CHRIST AND THE CHURCH"
by
Catherine Miller Balm

Part One—A Fruitful Thought

Scene   I—A Young Man's Proposal
Outside the Mission Sunday School, Abbott Village,
Massachusetts
1875

Scene II—A Young Man's Plan
The Parsonage, Williston Congregational Church,
Portland, Maine
1881

Interlude—Through the Years

Part Two—Into All the World

Scene   I—A Street in Tarsus, Turkey
1893

Scene II—A Chapel in the Village of Chabikabar, India
1896

Scene III—A Street in London
1900

Scene IV—Youth Camp at Balatonszarzo, Hungary
1930

Scene V—The Road to the Leper Colony, Endeavor Village, Luebo, Belgian Congo,
Africa
1938

Scene VI—A Cave in Rural China
1941

Interlude—Join Hearts with Joy

Part Three—Into All of the Life of Youth

Scene   I—Planning—The Christian Endeavor Union Board Room
Evening

Scene II—Serving —The Corridor of the City Mission
Christmas Eve

Scene III—Playing —The Social Hall of First Church
Evening

Scene IV—Praying —A Quiet Place Anywhere
Early Morning

Scene V—Praising —A Lakeside
Twilight

Finale—"This Is Christian Endeavor's Jubilee"

CAST OF CHARACTERS

Part One

Scene I—Harriet Elizabeth Abbott
Members of the congregation
Francis E. Clark

Scene II—The Reverend Francis E. Clark
Mrs. Francis E. Clark
W. H. Pennell
Other young people

First Interlude

Christian Endeavorers of six decades

Part Two

Scene I—Aram, president of the Junior Christian Endeavor society
His father
A beggar
Two women
Three soldiers

Scene II—Dr. Francis E. Clark
Young men and women of India

Scene III—First young man from the United States
Second young man from the United States
A flower woman
A cabman

Scene IV—Zoltan Cszorba ⎫ Hungarian Christian
Karolyi Dobos ⎬ Endeavor leaders
Emil Sander ⎭
Andrew Simon, from the United States
Emil Simon, his brother
Young men campers

(Note: The motto on the poster, in Hungarian, reads: "My heart a flame for Christ." This was the motto of John Calvin, and is the motto of the Hungarian Christian youth.)

Scene V—Two African bearers
Two African hammock carriers
An African child, a leper
His father ⎫ lepers
His mother ⎭
An American medical missionary

Second Interlude

Christian Endeavorers of many nations

Part Three

Scene   I—Young men and women on the Christian Endeavor Union Board

Scene II—A little girl, an orphan
          A little boy, an orphan
          Christian Endeavorers

Scene III—High School (Intermediate) Endeavorers

Scene IV—A Christian Endeavor president

Scene V—Christian Endeavorers

This pageant was produced under the direction of Catherine Miller Balm, Recreation Superintendent of the International Society of Christian Endeavor, by the Philadelphia Christian Endeavor Union, Henry M. Bates, president. Chairman of pageant committee, Louis J. Klein, Jr. Chorus director, Raymond L. Lyons.

The Delegation from the District of
Columbia brought much applause

IX

From the Diary of John Doe, Jr.

WELL, sir, there's one sure thing about keeping a diary during a Christian Endeavor Convention. And that is, you can't do it! There's more happening than you ever guessed could be crowded between breakfast and bedtime. There isn't a minute left to write down what is happening.

Phil Wray said, "Well, why bother trying to?" He told me there would be an official Convention Report, so why waste time keeping a diary?

I just grinned and didn't answer. I don't want anybody snickering at my Life's Ambition, which is to be a foreign correspondent. But how do I get to be one if I don't practice writing down what happens—especially when there's so much news right in front of me?

So I sat up Wednesday night, to get my record up to date—and yawned therefore during Quiet Hour Thursday morning, and Florence looked horrified. So I didn't stay up any later than I had to for the next two nights, and last night—well, Florence and Ruth and Jim and I took a walk to talk things over. So here's what was set down, and just a "reminder amount" on each event. (And mostly it didn't get written until Monday, when I'm waiting for Dad to drive in and take me back home to Boston.)

DIDN'T expect to like Quiet Hour so much! You had to get up awfully early to be in the Assembly Hall on time, but I did like it. Dr. Sockman spoke on Thursday morning on "Jesus, Prince and Pioneer." He had some ideas that made you think. I liked Dr. Blackwelder on Friday and Saturday, too. And Harry N. Holmes' sermon on Sunday morning. Boy, he's something, that fellow from New Zealand and Australia! Full of fun sometimes, and then sometimes serious enough to make the shivers go up and down your spine.

First I thought I was favored to get such good conference leaders. Then I began to hear the same thing from everybody else I talked to. All of them must have known their stuff, and they surely knew where young people live and what they're interested in talking about.

Is Martin Harvey keen! I took "A Christian's Efforts Toward Peace" on Thursday, and he was the leader. He used to be president of the

Christian Youth Council of North America; he's a Negro and most members of the Council are white, so that was a real tribute to a real man. Saturday I was studying and discussing "How to Have Better Meetings" with Richard Hoiland as leader. I began to load a notebook with those ideas—ideas that'll make our society grow right out of the meeting-room, for they'll certainly make things hum.

Thursday afternoon, a bunch of us played ball on the beach and swam. What a beach! Then we hurried back to the hotel to dress for the High School Banquet. All through the Convention there were lots of special luncheons and banquets and dinners. Yet I think none of them was as much fun as our banquet, and the price didn't get you down either!

At that High School Banquet, we had 150 enthusiastic young people from all points East and West in the banquet hall of the Hotel Monticello. Dr. Raymond Veh, who directed the High School Division of the Convention, and a big job that was, presided at this dinner and led the group singing. The tables vied with one another to present original songs.

Between the courses we heard readings and musical dialogues by Dr. and Mrs. W. H. Detweiler and Claire Pfeiffer. D. Charles Davies, the International Society's special representative, sang Negro spirituals, accompanied by Mrs. Mahoney. Then China took things over in fine style. Mrs. Philip Lee talked, and was she fun! Then Mr. Lee gave a longer talk and also sang solos. We heard him again in the big pageant.

Thursday night was thrilling. Joy Homer told about her trip to China and how the Chinese young people are doing heroic deeds under the leadership and example of Christian missionaries and the Chinese Christian people. Dr. Herbert Gezork, who was a Christian youth leader in Germany till "that man" took over, told about how devoted the young "Nasties" and Communists are to their leaders—and what that ought to mean to us who are Christians. If we want to overcome the evils that have gripped Europe, we'll have to care and dare a lot more for Jesus and for Christianity.

Yes, the Massachusetts "good night" Quiet Hour was pretty serious, coming right after that. We have a job to do.

FRIDAY brought me a big thrill! Mrs. Balm, who wrote and directed the Rainbow Jubilee Pageant, asked me to take the place of a fellow who was in the pageant but had been called home because his Dad got very sick. So I went to pageant rehearsal in the afternoon; found myself a Hungarian Christian Endeavorer in a camp with a name like a sneeze. But Mrs. Balm says Balatonszarzo is one of the beauty spots of Europe, a plateau looking out over blue Lake Balaton. Rich people would go there from Budapest for the summer, but the fellows in the camp were very poor. I liked the part when I began to get the "feel" of this young Hungarian member of C. E.

Dad had warned me not to miss the big Convention Banquet, which also came on Friday. I might have gone to the Steel Pier instead, but I am glad I went to this banquet, the biggest party I've ever attended. Thousands were there, I suppose. The girls had their long swishy dresses; they wore flowers in their hair. We had a sea-food dinner, and we sang, sang, and sang. Rody led. Norman Klauder presided, introducing all the celebrities—like the Polings, Mrs. Helen Lyon Jones, Harry Holmes, lots of others. Philip Lee sang; that pleased everyone. We'd been telling folks about this Chinese preacher's voice since the High School Banquet, when we came to know him. Mr. Espy spoke about young people in Europe; we could have listened much longer, for he was easy to take. As a foreign correspondent I would like to interview people who know the other lands like this leader does.

When we marched up the Boardwalk to the Assembly Hall, those Florida delegates were practicing a trick step to use in the parade next day. They were strung out across the Boardwalk and sort of spelling *Florida* with heel and toe taps. That took practice!

We'll remember the Friday night session because it introduced us to our new and pretty Associate President, Pauline Shoemaker, of Washington, D. C. And we met a big basket of flowers, too. That was a human interest story all by itself.

When Dr. Poling announced Miss Shoemaker's election and introduced her, the District of Columbia delegates sent down an immense basket of flowers. (We saw it again in the parade next day.) She thanked them, put the flowers down—and the basket was top-heavy and rolled over. Out came lots of water. Dr. Vandersall went after that with a mop that stood handy in the wings, and the ever-helpful Briggs of the Auditorium staff helped, too.

So everybody felt very relaxed and human. Florence nearly choked with laughter, and we thought our whole row might be chased from the hall—but then there was applause for the other officers Dr. Poling presented. More comedy came with the flowers that Pennsylvania presented to each one of its leaders who were being elected or appointed to office, and there were several. The State President, Bert Shaw, and the Field Secretary, Warren Hoopes, gave a kiss with each bouquet, like a French general of the old days handing out the medals in a news-reel.

We were laughing when Dr. Norman V. Peale, just in from the airport and from Hollywood, was presented. He took us in his stride. Everyone felt gay, and then suddenly he had us thinking and serious, and maybe worried. Christian Endeavor Conventions are like that. You feel you are a part of life and that you can do something about it. C. E. is called a movement, and it moves!

Saturday morning was like other mornings with its conference program, except we hated to think it was the last chance at conferences and High School assemblies (or Convocations—$10 word!). Over two hundred of us enjoyed those Convocations; they were very informal, with fun and fellowship at the close of each morning's session. Dr. Veh led these periods, using the delegates for all sorts of activities. We met in the High School Auditorium, thanks to Mrs. Detweiler and other good friends in Atlantic City.

Well, we sang pep songs and ballads this morning, and Negro spirituals. Then came announcements, and the Question Box was opened next. Aided by other conference leaders, Dr. Veh went through the whole list; most were about Christian Endeavor organization and methods, how to have better meetings, world issues, but there were many good ones (well answered) about questions of personal conduct.

Mrs. Greene's group of Washington young people led the Wednesday worship period following the discussion; Mrs. Camp's group from Atlantic City had this period on Thursday.

THEY don't parade on the Boardwalk! Convention after convention comes here and strolls along the promenade, but we *marched* on it, by permission of the city government, drove cars on it, played band music, tapped out Florida's name, and all the rest. Not that this was a snake-dance or football-victory celebration. The parade was serious. It impressed people; you could see that all along the line. It was a good parade, and Massachusetts drew lots of applause with its Pilgrim marchers who were carrying bells (church bells, school bells, or curfew?).

I was in only one little scene of the pageant (Part Two, Scene IV), so maybe in this Convention diary I can praise what the others did. Florence and Jim and Phil said it was gr-r-rand!

This started late because Dr. Poling was giving the delegates a chance to make pledges for Christian Endeavor's support. There was a huge sixtieth-anniversary birthday cake with electric candles, and when $1,000 was pledged, the tall center candle named for Mother Clark was lighted.

Well, when the pageant began there were about five thousand people in the audience and that was a big enough crowd for me. Did my knees shake!

The Philadelphia Christian Endeavor Union had recruited most of those who took part. They'd rehearsed in Philadelphia, and the costumes and props came from their city, too. Louis J. Klein, Jr., was chairman of the pageant committee and Lena Schubert was in charge of make-up. She worked hard behind the scenes.

THE first part of the pageant showed Dr. and Mrs. Clark getting engaged on a rainy evening after prayer-meeting. Then it was six years later, the minister and his wife were still young and not at all famous, and the first Christian Endeavor society was being planned and organized in the parsonage at Portland, Maine, where Francis Clark was steadily building up a Congregational church.

Then came a procession called "Through the Years," showing Endeavorers from 1881 till now. There were some queer clothes worn in 1881 and in 1911 and even in 1920, when Mother and Dad were leaders in Christian Endeavor. The men's suits were especially funny, and you should have seen Norman Klauder with whiskers!

While the interest of the audience grew, for there was nothing draggy in this whole pageant, our cast showed exciting Christian Endeavor events all over the world. Why, Christian Endeavor had real heroes to present— some who died for their faith!

Then we saw the youth movement going about its work today. The vespers scene, supposed to be outdoors, with the light changing from sunset to starlight, was one of those "Oh!" and "Ah!" spectacles. I'd have been glad to see it from the audience seats.

I believe we could repeat most of that pageant in our church home, or all of it if we wanted to, and it would be fun to see if we could work out such good costumes and lighting.

A big chorus sang between scenes and also during the second procession, "Christian Endeavor in All Lands." The chorus came from Philadelphia especially to help in this pageant. Marshall Noack, who is the minister of music in Dr. Poling's Philadelphia church, sang two solos; he has a wonderful voice. A quintette of Negro young men sang fine, too.

Dr. Poling said, "The pageant was glorious in conception and beautiful in its presentation," and he thanked Mrs. Balm very eloquently.

Our state had a questionnaire to fill out, now that the Convention was nearing the end. It asked, "Which speakers were most inspiring?" and "What would you like to have changed in the next Convention?" To that one, we said we'd like them to arrange not to have any last day!

But the last day was glorious and happy after all. I'll never forget our early morning communion service, with thousands of delegates of all denominations being served together. And the morning church service was very inspiring. Rev. Arthur J. Stanley, who was the first Associate President of recent years, now Vice-President, was in charge, and Mr. Holmes preached the sermon.

All of our crowd got together for dinner at the hotel. In the afternoon we went to Assembly Hall to hear Rev. Vere W. Abbey speak about India. We'd talked with him and Mrs. Abbey in the exhibition booth where all their things from India could be seen. When Mr. Abbey told you what Christian Endeavor does in India, you wanted to give your last dime to help work like that.

Then there was the noted Negro minister, Dr. William Lloyd Imes of New York, telling us what the Negro does for America. I was glad to hear this fine talk. We can quote parts of it in our next meeting on inter-racial goodwill.

Florence and I took a walk before supper, then had supper with the crowd. And now everyone was rushing off for the Christian Endeavor meetings, which are just about the best of their kind and show how good a meeting led by young people can be. Ours was the High School Christian Endeavor society meeting, with a program planned by Wallace Shipp and other Washington delegates.

It began with a musical prelude. Then this call to worship:

"If any man serve me, let him follow me; and where I am, there also shall my servant be. If any man serve me, him will my Father honor."

We sang "All Hail the Power of Jesus' Name," and the Scripture was Psalm 144:9-15.

Many of the delegates offered sentence prayers, and then there was a violin solo we liked. A panel discussion by seven speakers followed, and Rev. Daniel K. Poling ("Young Dan") summed up the viewpoints. We sang "We Choose Christ" and united in the Mizpah benediction.

NOW we were in the last Convention session—the very finish. And I'll remember it *always*. Dr. Louis Evans of California was just the man to stab souls awake. You want to do everything you can for Jesus and do it right now.

Of course there should be a decision service then, and so there was. We bowed our heads and prayed and thought of what we had heard and seen here, and we formed whatever decision we felt we were led to make for Christ. They said afterward that 1,071 different young people in the Convention made and signed personal decisions: 380 accepting Jesus as their personal Saviour, 325 declaring for full-time service for Him, while hundreds also came out as tithers or soul-winners or volunteers for any Christian service that might open in their church or their community.

My decision was—I'll take a teacher-training course beginning in the fall, so I can teach a Sunday school class.

At the end, all of us clasped hands and sang "God Be With You Till We Meet Again." And we went out from the Convention with the pledge in our hearts to do all things "Always—For Christ and the Church."

X

Ring That Bell

It's Town Meeting Time

THE Town Crier's bell began to ring. You heard only the first clear "ding-dong!" For no sooner did Associate President Lawrence W. Bash appear with the Town Meeting bell than the burst of applause from the delegates would drown out every other sound.

Christian Endeavor's Town Meeting was a decidely popular program feature.

Lawrence Bash explained the purpose at the first of the four sessions, on Wednesday morning. The Town Meeting would give the delegates a chance to consider some of the pressing problems which young people are facing. Each morning several young persons presented their points of view and made concrete suggestions about the solution of a youth problem. Each speaker was strictly limited to four minutes. When this pre-arranged program was completed delegates were invited to come to the platform to carry along a free-for-all discussion of youth's problems. From Wednesday through Saturday morning, many of the young people gladly accepted this opportunity to express their opinions in the Rainbow Jubilee Convention of International Christian Endeavor.

There follow some of the statements made by the young people who addressed the Town Meeting. (Many of the same group of outstanding young Endeavorers took part also in a Wednesday night event, as some of the "Voices of Other Lands" that added another real note of drama to Dr. Poling's thrilling Presidential Address.)

Youth and the Alcohol Problem

W. Roy Breg, Jr.

We have a great problem facing America today: the alcohol problem. Today more money is spent on alcohol in these United States than on education. The present crisis makes an even greater problem than we ordinarily have. For instance, did you know that beer is being sold to the men in the Army camps by the United States government? Mind you, by our own government! Is this preparing to defend America? And of course more liquor is being sold outside the camps. Since more money is being circulated, more liquor is being bought.

Now you may say: "Something must be done. We can't have this!"

But what do you do? Many times, nothing is done. Yet there are a few organizations that are doing something. One of these is Allied Youth. Through education it is helping young people in high schools to make their own decisions about alcohol. Their platform is: "We stand for the liberation, through education, of the individual and society from the handicaps of beverage alcohol."

Here are several things you might do through Christian Endeavor societies. You

87

can encourage your high school to have an Allied Youth Post. Information may be secured from Allied Youth headquarters, in the National Education Association Building, Washington, D. C. You can help the fellows in the Army to have a good time when they are on leave, without having alcohol enter the picture. Encourage legislation against alcohol. Write your Senator; tell him what you want.

At the Christian Endeavor Convention here in 1911, a resolution was passed for a saloonless nation by 1920. And did they have it? Sure they had it! I challenge you young people and you older people to take a similar stand today.

Conflict Between Church and School

RUTH HAVERSTOCK

In Prince George County, Maryland, the schools give one hour a week to religious education. In Washington one school gives its assembly period to a minister.

Christian Endeavor can make interesting speakers available and use every opportunity to place them in the schools.

Church colleges are another problem. Sometimes there is no college-age society in the college chapel.

I challenge those in churches in college towns to give students who come from Christian homes what Christian Endeavor can give them.

The Problem of Leisure Time

MARY ELLEN PERRY

A problem which seems very vital to me, in regard to community life, is the prob lem of leisure time. This is called "scientific America"—let us pause for a moment and look at our own lives. Does each person spend his leisure time as a Christian should? If he does, I wonder that we have thousands of taverns, night clubs filled with young people, and so much interest in so-called glamour life. I wonder that we have 1,350,000 girls engaged in the distribution of liquor, with a host of lives lost each year because the liquor traffic and gambling lead to the disintegration of morals. So we see that the harvest is great. Let us start putting into practice the stewardship of time.

I think that each church should have an outstanding, attractive social program which will appeal to the young people. This program certainly has to be active, to keep up with the swing of the world today. There are so many ways to interest the young people, and the earlier the age we begin this program, the better. I know of one church whose minister meets with the young people once a week for a crafts class. Following this, they have a prayer-meeting. What an active Christian Endeavor society this is! Another church has a hobby club which meets every two weeks. My own church provides a tennis court for us and we also enjoy dramatic work.

Put into practice the things which we are discussing. We must see Christian Endeavor really in action. It is better to light a candle than to curse the darkness. May each one of us accept the responsibility to work on the stewardship of time for Christ and the church.

The Racial Problem

MIRIAM FEAVER

"Suffer little children to come unto me." Each one of us has seen the picture of our Master with a group of children, each of a different race, around Him. How many of us get off into our own racial corner? In the South on the way to this Convention I was disturbed by the sign, "Colored Waiting Room."

We Christian Endeavorers should do everything we can to make friends with other races. In politics all votes count. Socially, we go about in cliques. In God's sight all men are equal. In our town a church has missionary work for the Chinese and Japanese there. Instead, there should be an inter-racial Christian Endeavor society. We have invited the others to our society. The Japanese have come, and they invited us in turn. Spiritually we are all one; true Christian Endeavorers never consider race at all. We should try to get other young people to feel that we are all one, regardless of race. Personal prejudices should be stamped out.

Gambling Can Be Kept Out

W. D. SMITH, JR.

Christians are sometimes very self-righteous. Discussing what I do and won't do with a friend, I felt satisfied because I didn't do things he did. Later I said, "I'll match you for a 'coke.' " He said, "I don't gamble." I hadn't thought of that as gambling, but it was.

Huge sums are spent by church people on gambling, by people calling themselves Christians. As to the spiritual effects of gambling, you need only to see the wrecked lives it causes. We should take action against gambling. I was glad to see that the bingo games here had been closed down. There are no slot machines on the street corners in Birmingham any more. The church people banded together to keep them out.

Statements from Other Youth

The Kansas Christian Endeavor Union hung 400,000 door-knob hangers asking people to vote dry—for Christian youth. Kansas went dry.—*Mary Ellen Perry.*

Michigan decided to stop exploitation at the selling end. A bill prohibiting certain types of liquor advertising was introduced in the state legislature, with Christian Endeavor behind it. All the liquor interests converged to fight it. At a recent session, we got the bill through the Senate and into the House. It was stopped there by pressure, but we're going on working for it.—*Ernest S. Marks.*

We have a bill—S-860—in the Senate to prohibit sale of liquor in Army camps. I wish we could have two thousand letters to back it up.—*A Pennsylvania delegate.*

We put out 33,000 petitions against the liquor situation. We're trying to stop the sale of liquor at places where there is dancing.—*An Iowa delegate.*

Are we going to pass pious resolutions, or go home resolved to see that the liquor traffic passes from our shores?—*Chairman Bash.*

How can we stop gambling if we sell chances in the churches and have bingo games?—*A New Jersey delegate.*

Baltimore has an inter-racial fellowship several years old. We meet at a downtown church and attend services together. We try to patronize a restaurant to see if there is discrimination; so far we've not had much success in this line. We have our hikes and swims together. I wish Christian Endeavor could form an inter-racial fellowship in each town.—*A Maryland delegate.*

A most successful inter-racial fellowship is being conducted in Philadelphia. You can write to Dr. Fred D. Wentzel, 1505 Race Street, Philadelphia, to get details.—*A Pennsylvania leader.*

The Loyalty of Youth to the Church

DORIS MARKS

At any time on the Boardwalk, thousands of young people may be seen strolling along, apparently unconcerned with the responsibilities of the world. They seem to have only one idea in mind, that of having a good time. The youth of today often seem more interested in the latest style, or in movies, or things like that. There's a great need for a movement to reach young people for the church. For the last sixty years, Christian Endeavor has been helping to meet this problem and bring youth into the church of Christ.

In answer to the problem, a plan of organization has been made in Michigan. In most of our Christian Endeavor societies we have a church-activity committee. The idea is to carry our ideals into practice. The committee tries to stimulate members to participate in church work. The committee members are able to give the following services: (1) publicity, (2) ushering, (3) stenographic aid, (4) music, (5) church projects, (6) aid to pastor, (7) financial, planning a program and developing responsibility, (8) supply of leadership. There are so many ways that young people can help their church.

Through relationship with the leaders of the church we shall be developing goodwill and cooperation. Our societies are part of the church, and we owe our loyalty to this institution. Do we show our loyalty by regular attendance at church and by supporting the total program of the church? Let us remember that Christian Endeavor is an active, church-centered youth program. "Trusting in the Lord Jesus Christ for strength," let's keep it so,—for Christ and the *church!*

Training Leadership

Doris Poffenberger

How is the church going to get the very essential leadership that it needs to go forward? As we look around us at all the confusion in the world, there are brought to mind definite leaders of movements that are not connected with Christian organization. We can see that good Christian leadership is necessary. What would our Christian Endeavor movement be today if it were not for the dynamic leadership of our own President Poling? But how is the church going to get the necessary leaders? It is up to Christian Endeavor to train them.

The secret of Christian Endeavor is its way of placing responsibility upon young people, so that through doing they may learn. Training begins as soon as one enters the society. I learned, in one of the Intermediate conferences, that one Intermediate talks to each new member, defining for him the principles of Christian Endeavor and what it means to be an Endeavorer. Through the Christian Endeavor meetings we learn to express ourselves, to think things through, and to plan definite programs of action.

Outstanding young people become leaders and officers in their own societies. Some societies have definite responsibilities in the services of their church. My own society takes charge of the Mother's Day service. We are given the opportunity also to be ushers and to sing in the choir. Our leaders as they grow older and more experienced become leaders of missionary societies and teachers in the Sunday school. Some have received the call to become missionaries and ministers.

Leadership courses for high school groups tell them just what is expected. I challenge all Endeavorers to have such active societies that each member may have a chance to assume leadership.

Denominational Programs

Howard Duven

How can my society foster the program of my denomination and also participate in a wider fellowship with young people's groups of numerous denominations?

My denomination would not isolate itself from the motivating association with other Christian groups; but to fulfill its possibilities and responsibilities it is properly conscious of the necessity of training its youth and acquainting them with the denominational objectives.

But, you say, with two or more programs and organizations appealing for the young people's support, how are we going to choose? Shall we choose all of one, to the complete exclusion of the other? Or shall we blend the two into the program for our church? Examination of programs will show clearly that they are not set against each other, but that they supplement each other. Christian youth's responsibility to the world is certainly a desired aim of the denominations, and Christian Endeavor offers a way of reaching that aim.

A pastor of one of Iowa's largest churches—a church which was formed by the merging of two local congregations—makes this statement of solution: "We pour all suggested programs together. We take the cream off the top, and for the most part this whips up satisfactorily."

In most cases it is fully possible to remain a Christian Endeavor society and at the same time participate in denominational relationships. So we have a Christian Endeavor society in the Pilgrim Fellowship, or the Christian Youth Fellowship, and so forth. In the values of the larger association we urge societies to retain not only the name of Christian Endeavor in their respective denominational fellowship but to participate actively in Christian Endeavor's far-reaching program.

Christian Unity

Rosy Bulley

As we are gathered here today in the fellowship of Christian Endeavor, the difficulties of two hundred years ago seem impossible. Then, between the different churches, there were strife, bitterness, jealousy and envy, making difficult situations, preventing cooperation, and making help for world conditions impossible. How far we have moved! Today we have no place for unbrotherliness. Today in our Convention Communion Services, members of many denominations come gladly to the Lord's Supper together.

Cooperation between church groups is a necessity. Together we must face such problems as that of the migrants, liquor advertising, soldiers in camp, China relief. Together we must promote the National Preaching Mission. We see movements toward unity between denominations in the World Conference, in the merger of Northern and Southern Methodists and Methodist Protestants, in the merger of the Congregational and Christian churches, the Evangelical and Reformed churches, and the proposed merger of United Brethren and Evangelical Church.

Christian Endeavor has made a major contribution to this new understanding. It has demonstrated that the things upon which we agree are greater than those upon which we differ.

From Other Delegates

I believe in Christian Endeavor cooperation. The young people of First Presbyterian Church in Louisville are the biggest element in an ongoing church. We have Graded Christian Endeavor. The four other societies are supervised by the fifth, the Young People's society, because we have no paid director. Three years ago the front seats in church were always vacant. Now the young people as a group fill those seats instead of sitting in the back.—*Dr. Frank Anderson.*

A year ago our young people made a survey in Denver, in a territory one mile square. This was canvassed by one hundred young people who went to 5,000 homes to invite young people to the young people's society meetings and others to attend church. One society now has an average attendance of 130.—*A Colorado delegate.*

In Baptist Temple, Philadelphia, we have Daily Vacation Bible Schools for white children and Negro children. We have a Temple camp for young people. Our youth club is open every afternoon and evening for social fellowship.—*A Pennsylvania delegate.*

Our churches lean heavily on the young people. In many churches the Junior choir furnishes the music. Young people support prayer-meeting, act as ushers, and do secretarial work for the pastor.—*Rev. A. Z. Arnold, President of Maine Christian Endeavor Union.*

Our church was a failure and just about to close, when we were helped by Frances Sangster Huston [secretary to Dr. Poling]. She made us close up the bingo games, encouraged the young people to raise money in other ways to pay church debts. Now we have young people on the board of trustees, and two of them are deacons.—*A Pennsylvania delegate.*

Our Christian Endeavor society, started by one woman, now has thirty members. We take care of our society; we get along without the older folks—but sometimes we are glad to ask them for advice.—*A New Jersey delegate.*

I think that loyalty is due Christian Endeavor by the church. We can't expect to exist half C. E., half something else. We are Christian first! I believe that the young people should be given a chance to decide if they will be led by the adults into something else or be allowed to keep their Christian Endeavor heritage.—*Viola Gunther.*

A Summary by Dr. Poling

I am thrilled by what these speakers have said. Their experience, like mine, is that the young people are the most responsive in the church. We have no conflict with denominational life and activity; our society at home could not survive without the denominational leadership and fellowship. Our first allegiance is to Christ. With Him as our authority, we give first service to the church of which we are a part.

Ours is not a pulseless uniformity; it is a pulsing, dynamic movement. A postmaster in China told me that he was young in Christianity (he was forty-three years of age), but that Christian Endeavor was training him. It looked unlike Christian Endeavor to me, in its details, but it broke over me that we had a truer unity than could be expressed by details. Our unity is not in creeds, liturgies, race, but in Christ. The fact that we are Christian Endeavorers does not mean that we are less loyal to the church to which we belong; it makes us give more intelligent loyalty.

If we are to take the world for Christ, it will be because we go forward together.

Facing the National Emergency

Christian Endeavor encourages independent thinking. Christian Endeavor expects every member to follow Christ's will as that member sees it. This freedom of choice was shown most clearly in the last of the series of Town Meetings. The subject to be discussed was one on which widely divergent views are held, and the same thoughtful attention was given to every statement of personal conviction on the issue.

The draft, of course, was a controversial issue. One delegate spoke firmly in favor of accepting compulsory military service as an opportunity. Because of cynicism on the part of youth—he thought—the discipline of the training camp was needed. He felt that it was an educational advantage to meet young men from all parts of the nation. He felt, too, that here was a great opportunity for the church to reach young people. Nearby training camps are Christian Endeavor's evangelistic opportunity.

With equal fervor another fine delegate expressed his earnest convictions as a conscientious objector.

A particularly helpful contribution came from Harry Ray of

Georgia, representing a society which formed its own "defense program" to serve soldiers in a nearby post.

Christian Endeavor's Defense Program

HARRY RAY

Nine miles from the city of Columbus, Georgia, is the United States' largest infantry training school, Fort Benning. For years the people of Columbus looked upon Fort Benning merely as a nearby town or community. Along came the Selective Service Act, and young men from all walks of life literally poured into Columbus and Fort Benning.

At first the people of Columbus did not change their view of the military men. The boys, as a general rule, who went to the city churches were not given the warm clasp of Christian fellowship. They naturally felt that they were not welcome in the churches; they turned to the saloons, poolrooms, and bars. As a result, Columbus was finding itself morally degraded.

Things became worse. There was a tension growing between the so-called respectable civilians and those in Army life. Something had to be done to bring the boys who did not know what to do in such a position, and those who had drifted away, into the Christian fold.

I will try to give a brief outline of the program launched by our Christian Endeavor society, which has now grown into a city-wide movement.

Contacted Army chaplains with goodwill offers of assistance and service

Arranged with Army chaplains to present programs to the soldiers, and have continued doing this regularly. Soon received many invitations to present these.

Set up plan for regular parties or socials every other Friday night, with Christian Endeavorers entertaining selected groups of soldiers brought in by chaplains of various sections of the camp. We are continuing this work as a regular program, and through these socials have contacted many Christian Endeavorers, bringing them and others into our church activities while in this community.

At our Christian Endeavor Rainbow Jubilee Birthday Banquet, we entertained soldiers, chaplains, and other officers. Some took part in the program.

Set aside and observed Hospitality Day, when thousands of soldiers were entertained as guests in homes of citizens. Each family was asked to take three boys.

Arranged for many boys to be entertained in homes on Mother's Day.

Planned special parties such as wiener roasts, picnics, retreats, etc., to which we invite soldier friends.

Launched a program of the same nature at the nearby C. C. C. camp, which is also the largest camp of its kind. Activity for these boys has now also become a city-wide project.

Have invited different chaplains into our church as guest speakers in the pulpit (through permission of the official church board) and urged them to bring as many boys as possible with them to the service.

Have functioning committees to study and serve the needs applying to their committee for welcoming, entertaining, contacting, refreshments, etc.

We now have a well-organized program of activity, and are very happy in the work for these boys.

Some of you say, "I don't live near an army camp. What can I do?"

You can help a lot by writing your Christian friends who do live near camps, arranging to go and put on programs, plays, etc., constantly writing those you know who are now in Army life and helping them to keep Christian ties of fellowship.

We have been happy to have various groups come from Christian Endeavor societies in Atlanta with presentations, and these were also gratefully received at Fort Benning.

However, there are many camps whose population exceeds that of the nearby towns. In such cases there is so little to be done to help the soldier in outside activities, in comparison to the amount of work there is to do. Therefore, the United Service Organization has been formed, under the sponsorship of President Roosevelt, Secretary Knox, Secretary Stimson, and Federal Security Administrator McNutt. These gentlemen have asked the Y. M. C. A., National Catholic Community Service, Salvation Army, Jewish Welfare Board, Y. W. C. A., and National Travelers Aid Association to join in cooperative effort to deal with this situation.

The forces of prostitution and gambling are already actively engaged in promoting their vicious trades. The color of the client's skin makes no difference to them! The rate of disease is alarming. The boys in uniform are going into the towns, standing on street corners and at highway intersections, wondering what to do, where to go, and with no good friends to whom they may turn for needed companionship or advice, making them easy prey for vice. The homesick boy is often the one who is prey to these unworthy elements and activities which promote questionable recreation, and even vice.

Will we as Christian Endeavorers rise to the challenge that the soldiers concentrated in our communities thrust upon us?

Virginia, too, had something good to say about Richmond City Union's open house for service men.

Said Adeline Curry:

We have a camp of 22,000 soldiers near Richmond. The city has a big dance every Saturday night, which cares for a few thousand. But some of the boys do not dance and some others haven't the money for other amusements. Our city union has been holding open house at the Y. M. C. A. on Saturday nights. Punch and cake are served, and we play the piano and sing. Also we talk a lot together, which is what the boys really come for.

A different society takes charge every week. Just as the boys leave the "Y", one of our members gives out a copy of the Gospel According to St. John, for each service man to put into his pocket.

We have provided music and entertainment for activities in camp and are going to do a lot more of this in the future. Plans are under way to start a Christian Endeavor society at the reception center at Camp Lee.

What Defense Days Can Mean to Christian Endeavor

Gilmore B. Seavers

In our Rainbow Jubilee Convention, we are confronted with the call of national defense. In this Convention there has been much said and done which correctly and emphatically prefaces our action in this field. The instruction of our conferences should be taken back to our societies and unions, and this coupled with the challenge and inspiration of the messages and music will lead, yes, compel us to greater action. We must make the investment which has been made in us pay dividends when we return home.

Here are some of the things which we can do. What about that society in your church which has been simply struggling under failing circumstances? You are going to go back and make that a better society because of the ideas which you have received from the fine conferences of this Convention. You are going to abandon the worst and weakest feature of society meetings: that is, you are going to do away with poor programs. Through better programs and better publicity you will build up that society into a worthwhile and successful organization.

What about that Sunday school class which has been needing a teacher? Now you are going to answer willingly, "Yes," and cooperate by doing what you can in this connection. Most particularly, you are going to assist your minister as never before in the program of the church, to make that essential part of the church's program more successful. May I be specific? Over in Pennsylvania, in an *alive* church with an *alive* pastor, this was tried not long ago. Leaders in the church, adults and young people alike, cooperated with the pastor by assuming the responsibility of filling a certain pew in the church auditorium on a certain Sunday, in what was called a full-pew contest. Through this procedure that church was filled both in the morning and in the evening. You can do this and many other things to help build up the pastor's program in your church.

Likewise most important will be our living, our witnessing, and our example, for through these we shall effect a constructive means to the end in point one. Then, too, we must remember that sin is a reproach to any nation but that righteousness exalts it. The great social issues of the day demand our attention. We must do everything we can in our respective communities to abolish or at least mitigate the evils in connection with drinking, gambling, the pulp-paper magazines, and the desecration of the Sabbath. Herein we will continue to cooperate with the Allied Youth movement.

In all these things let us turn our resolutions into programs, actions, and accomplishments.

Martin L. Harvey — Dr. Poling — Herbert L. Minard

XI

The Gist of Many Conferences

THE educational conferences of the Atlantic City Convention were arranged in two age-group divisions, as follows: (1) for Young People (18 years of age and over); (2) for the High School ages (under 18).

The emphasis for the first two days, Wednesday and Thursday, was on the word *Christian*, and the conferences held from 9:25 to 10:35 each of these mornings were largely concerned with the interpretation and enlargement of Christian principles.

The plan of the 1941 Convention enrolled each delegate in a given conference group for two days in sequence, so that the group was together in all for nearly two hours and a half, and a thorough consideration of the subject could take place.

These were the subjects and leaders for Wednesday and Thursday mornings:

YOUNG PEOPLE'S DIVISION

What does it mean to be Christian?	Dr. Manson Doyle
The church in today's world	Rev. Vere W. Abbey
Enriching the worship of Christian Endeavor	Dr. Frank D. Getty
Working with other races and creeds	Dr. Robert W. Gammon
Accepting the challenge of citizenship	W. Roy Breg
A Christian's efforts toward peace	Ernest R. Bryan
Christian missions today	Mrs. Vere W. Abbey
Preparation for home and marriage	Rev. Clifford Earle
Making the most of leisure time	Moses M. Shaw
Christian Endeavor in the total program of the church	Dr. J. Arthur Heck
What are Christian Endeavor essentials?	Rev. George R. Sweet
A Christian's duty to the state	Dr. George Oliver Taylor
Vocational decisions for youth	Arch J. McQuilkin
Relationship of Christian Endeavor to other agencies for youth, Rev. Arthur J. Stanley	

HIGH SCHOOL DIVISION

What does it mean to be Christian?	Rev. Elmer Becker
Overcoming our prejudices	Rev. Herbert L. Minard
Problems in personal conduct	Luther R. Medlin
A Christian's efforts toward peace	Martin L. Harvey, Jr.
What can we do as citizens?	P. Marion Simms, Jr.
Sharing life and possessions	Rev. James A. Thomas
What are Christian Endeavor essentials?	Mrs. L. C. Greene

On Friday and Saturday mornings the emphasis of the educational conferences shifted to the word *Endeavor*, and now the "school of the Convention" enrolled the young people and younger delegates for the study and discussion of the development of Christian action and organization.

As in the earlier program of the conferences, the leadership was shared by both denominational leaders of young people's work and the employed and volunteer officers of state unions and cooperating organizations that work with the churches.

YOUNG PEOPLE'S DIVISION

Meeting membership problems	D. Charles Davies
Better Christian Endeavor meetings (A)	Geneva F. Craig
Better Christian Endeavor meetings (B)	Dr. George Oliver Taylor
Society officers at work	P. Marion Simms, Jr.
Worship in the Christian Endeavor society	Rev. Clifford Earle
Methods of living devotionally	Rev. Herbert L. Minard
How to organize a Christian Endeavor society	Warren G. Hoopes
Reaching others for Christ	Dr. S S Morris
Publicity that gets results	Rev James A Thomas
World outreach for the society	Rev. George H. Wilson
Getting results from alcohol education	W Roy Breg
How can the society help the church?	Moses M. Shaw
The Christian as a steward	Rev. Gene Stone
Christian Endeavor for adults	Rev Ellis R Shaw

HIGH SCHOOL DIVISION

How to have better meetings	Rev. Richard A Holland
A complete program for every society	Rev. Arthur J. Stanley
Reaching others for Christ	Luther R. Medlin
What makes the society go?	Rev. Al Goodrich
How can the society help the church?	Mrs. Reba Rickman
Devotional practices for young Endeavorers	Rev Roy Schreiner
Getting the most out of leisure time	Dorothy Lehman

Special interests of delegates, including ministers who attended the Convention in numbers, were well recognized in four special conferences which were arranged on a four-day basis.

The fellowship of prayer	*Leader,* Mrs. Lillian D. Poling
	Chairman, Pauline Shoemaker
How to get the most out of the Bible	*Leader,* Dr. Frederick W Cropp
	Chairman, Rev. Gene Stone

Making Christian Endeavor unions successful

Leader, Ernest S. Marks
Assisted by Rev. George R. Sweet, Warren G. Hoopes, D. Charles Davies, and others

Conference for pastors, directors of young people's work, and other professional leaders   *Leader,* Dr. Daniel A. Poling
Chairman, Dr. J. Gordon Howard

The Junior workers' division conducted the following sessions for state and provincial Junior superintendents and for Junior workers and leaders in societies and unions:

WEDNESDAY

Facing Forward. A combined conference and fellowship period for all society and union Junior workers.
"Let's know each other," Dorothy Kling.
"The coming program and its use with Juniors," Dr. Stanley B. Vandersall.

THURSDAY

Increasing our membership. For society and union Junior workers. Leader, Sara McCloy. Chairman, M. Virginia Hopkins.
State and Provincial Junior Superintendents' Discussion. Leader, Dorothy Kling.

FRIDAY

Improving our meetings. Leader, Dorothy Kling.
Superintendents' Discussion. Leader, Mrs. Juanita C. Elder.

SATURDAY

Sharing with others. Leader, Mrs. Vere W. Abbey.
Superintendents' Discussion. Leader, Sara McCloy.

A wealth of material represents those Convention conferences in the records that leaders, chairmen, and conference secretaries have placed with the International Society. Some of this material will be quoted in *The Christian Endeavor World* during the period in which societies and unions are actively promoting and conducting the 1941-1943 program, "Always—For Christ and the Church." The gist of many successful hours spent together by thousands of Endeavorers and leaders must be compressed here into a few pages—but we believe you will enjoy and profit by the selection that has been made from the many conference reports.

Only the leader's name can be given in the printing of these quotations. The conference leaders gladly give credit to delegates who shared in these sessions for adding many of the comments and raising numerous questions that increased and deepened the total educational value of the group gatherings.

Being a Christian

What are our sources of help concerning Christian living? Delegates chose (in order of importance) Christian home life, corporate worship, personal experience. Mentioned also were New Testament, biographies, current literature (religious and secular), radio, visual aids, personal contacts, organized and united Christian groups, Christian hymns.

Test of Christianity: the conviction of one's own conscience, tested by the judgment of the Bible and of the church.

Anywhere, any time, any Christian person will show distinctive marks or qualities: faith in Christ, working of supernatural upon one's life, love of God and man, obedience to God, a creative Christian personality (created by the transforming power of Christ and strengthened by His indwelling presence).

How to make Christ real to oneself: practice of the presence of God, either in the morning watch, or in the noon hour, or upon retiring.

—*Dr. Manson Doyle*

Our conference studied the Christian church and its various branches. There were about twenty denominations represented in the group. What were the fundamental differences? We discovered these:

(a) Baptism. Some immerse; some do not.
(b) Lord's Supper. Sacrament with some; ordinance or symbol with others.
(c) Polity. (Episcopal, presbyterian, or congregational.)
(d) Ritual. (High church, broad, low.)
(e) Theological differences other than these were rather individual than denominational.

Then, where did we agree?

(a) God, as Father and Creator.
(b) Jesus, Son of God and Saviour.
(c) Holy Spirit—Person of the Trinity, God in us.
(d) Sacraments: Baptism and Lord's Supper.
(e) Bible. Word of God with the plan of salvation.
(f) Church. Body of Christ; earthly organization through which we can realize His Kingdom. Therefore we are all responsible for missions, social service, Kingdom program.

"Likenesses are so much more important than differences that we should be able to work together."

Recommended book: "The Church of Our Fathers," by Prof. Roland H. Bainton.

Racial problems and the multiplicity of young people's organizations were considered. The "competition" among youth organizations was deprecated.

—*Rev. Vere W. Abbey.*

Christian Endeavor should not simply function within a church, but should be a church function. The group viewed the "total program of the church" from the standpoint of experiences of persons, relations of persons, departments of church work (worship, instruction, service, recreation), and denominational objectives. Christian Endeavor must discover ways in which it can work helpfully and constructively with every other organization in the local church.

The group suggested: "Operate meetings separately, but have common fellowship programs for different organizations. All interested in missions, for instance, could combine some activities." "Christian Endeavor should minister to every age group." "Christian Endeavor is the action department of the church." —*Dr. J. Arthur Heck.*

We must have plenty of work to do, in order to have a more powerful and growing society. A choir should be organized and participate in church services. We should help with the giving. Union of churches and young people's societies will serve the community. Societies should operate throughout the summer. An executive committee meeting should be held at least twice a month. Remember that the meetings of Christian Endeavor are for worship and fellowship.

The society may help its church in these ways: Attend church worship services; take charge of the evening service; provide a Junior choir; hold sunrise service, social service games, entertainments; help migrants; provide dramatics; start a library; financing; conduct nursery; help with mimeograph; make posters; clean the church; meet strangers after services; provide a bulletin board; help at church suppers.

—*Moses M. Shaw.*

It is sometimes a mistake to appoint a big committee. When God wanted a great task accomplished, He sent one person. At one time He sent His Son. We should impress personal responsibility on Endeavorers: teach them to know their jobs, urge them to fully prepare.

We can get spiritual strength through communion with God, through prayer and meditation. Spiritual strength is the greatest essential of Christian Endeavor.

—*Rev. Gene Stone.*

Cooperating With Other Agencies

After general discussion of question and purpose of the group we decided to list the various agencies under discussion, as follows:

Christian organizations: United Christian Youth Movement; Student Christian Youth Movement; Student Volunteer Movement; Young Men's Christian Association; Young Women's Christian Association; World Conference of Christian Youth; Hi-Y; Tri Hi-Y.

Miscellaneous organizations: Boy Scouts; Girl Scouts; 4-H Clubs; Future Farmers of America; United Service Organizations; Allied Youth; W. C. T. U.; fraternities; sororities; American Youth Congress.

Practically all denominations have a Young People's department, and many have an individual Young People's organization.

QUESTIONS

1. How can we cooperate with the United Christian Youth Movement?

(a) The U. C. Y. M. program and purpose is somewhat different from the C. E. set-up in that it is primarily for the older, more highly educated group and is primarily concerned with social issues and with education of the individual and the group, whereas Christian Endeavor is concerned with religious and world issues and seeks to train, through doing, in service of the church.

(b) There is more individual responsibility in the ramified C. E. organization program of departmental divisions.

(c) The local leadership of the Youth Council is not apt to be informed nor contagiously enthusiastic.

(d) The International Society of Christian Endeavor's attitude toward the United Christian Youth Movement is one of complete cooperation and purpose.

(e) We cannot be in competition, but must maintain spirit of sharing and understanding between the two groups.

2. How can we cooperate with the various denominational programs for youth?

(a) We must understand the purpose the denominations have in enlarging their youth work in seeming competition with Christian Endeavor.

(b) Denominational youth work is necessary to maintain the youth loyalty to the church.

(c) Denominations are creating youth fellowships to make all the youth groups in the denomination under one department. Despite the fact that many pastors and local leaders dismiss Christian Endeavor because of the enlarged denominational program, the larger organizations which cover the nation are cooperating fully with all denominational national offices and youth departments, and vice versa.

(d) **We should work out** our local programs with consideration of suggestions from all the youth agencies as to their purpose and program.

—*Rev. Arthur J. Stanley.*

Christian Endeavor Unions

The union program should be developed for an entire year. The program should include all the departmental service and emphases of Christian Endeavor which have a relation to the societies to be served. A program planning committee of union leaders may project plans during July and August to be ready for a full year's service beginning in September.

Christian intelligence rather than sentiment should govern our selection and retention of union officers. The welfare of the entire union is the first consideration. The nominating committee should be familiar with the duties of each office and should inform prospective officers fully, having their consent to serve before names are presented to the society.
—*Ernest S. Marks.*

When organizing a society, start with a small group. Help the group feel that they are organizing themselves, not being organized. "Christian Endeavor Essentials" and the "Program Guide" are needed by every society. The International Society's "Organizing Packet" is a necessity.

You do not need elaborate preparations for banding together as a Christian Endeavor group in college. Any small room at college can be used. You can worship in a small group in a quiet place.
—*Warren G. Hoopes.*

To Aid Our Endeavor

Why do we worship? We establish through worship a personal relationship to God and a Christlike fellowship among men, through which the worshipper shares God in spirit and purpose and receives strength for Christian living. Worship does not stop with the "Amen." It continues in our lives and in all things we do in life.

How? Prepare in advance, particularly for group worship. Have a purpose in the worship program. Purposes may be praise, adoration, love, thanksgiving or gratitude, loyalty or courage. Put the purposes into the form of a theme. Secure unity: by unity, the whole program of worship moves steadily and concisely toward your purpose or point of climax. The end, however, should not be too abrupt.

How begin the worship service? Soft music, a call to worship, silent prayer, announcement of the theme of the service.

Hymns for worship. Test a hymn by these elements: Does it have a Christian message? Is it good literature? Is it good music? Is it singable?

Scripture may be presented by drama. You may outline briefly the setting of the Scripture, then read only the portion pertaining to the worship theme.

Public worship needs atmosphere or setting. At all times a Bible, flowers, pictures, orderly arrangement of the room will help.

Centralize the program around the leader. Have participation, but always let the leader control and guide. Never let the program get out of hand and wander.
—*Dr. Frank D. Getty.*

A group of about twenty-five studied visual education. The group saw the film, "Hills and the Sea," intended for use in an evening worship program. Appropriate Scripture readings were proposed. The group was asked to suggest other familiar passages of Scripture which the film brought to mind.

In the second session, the group considered the use of the film, "The Kindled Flame," for a Young People's Society meeting. Reference was made to definite topics planned for 1942, for which this would be appropriate. Staying past adjournment time, the group also saw "Honesty Is the Best Policy." Some disagreed with the ending of the film, and the leader showed how well the discussion that followed had deepened the thought on this subject—which is the chief function of the life-situation type of film.   —*William L. Rogers.*

Look at the world situation from this angle: The world situation is not a Jewish problem but a Gentile one. The Jews introduced a moral social order when the Gentiles had none.

In working with other races and creeds, what can Christianity offer?

To make better human beings. To secure economic adjustment and social change. To provide a common ethical standard. To create a church which is more conscious of world needs. To foster a sense of personality responsibility so that each person thinks of a problem as being his own, as a part of the Christian community.
                                                          —*Dr. Robert W. Gammon.*

No one can name five or even two major causes of traffic accidents without including alcohol. Health is one of the chief sufferers from drinking. A Boston judge finds 90 per cent of misdemeanor cases in Massachusetts show a relationship to alcohol; 50 per cent of penal cases are so related. By the senior year in high school, from 43 per cent to more than 52 per cent of young people have made a beginning in drinking.

Allied Youth, an educational movement, not a prohibition organization, works particularly in high schools but also in communities. A few of its Posts are being started in colleges, as an outcome of young people coming up through the high schools and appreciating this program. More than 50,000 young people in high schools have participated in Allied Youth conferences; sometimes leaders of drinking groups respond. Athletes are quickest to respond to the Allied Youth idea, helping fellow students to organize this alcohol education program along voluntary lines and providing alcohol-free recreation to show how little the youth need beer and other drinks in order to have fun and be popular.

An important part of Allied Youth's purpose is to give young people a good time without drinking.

For society study and discussion: what famous coaches say; alcohol in relation to the human body; drinking in relation to safety; drinkers in industry. *The Allied Youth*, monthly except August, $1 a year, has many helps.   —*W. Roy Breg.*

Studying "A Christian's Efforts Toward Peace," one conference group commented on test statements to rate itself concerning the prejudices that are firmly held, including many planted by false propaganda. Such prejudices cause misunderstanding and hatred, and may lead to war.

Some of the members of the group favored a "World History Book," to be prepared by an international commission, which would present truth about the nations. Unfortunately each country has a sense of superiority. The United States thinks of itself as morally superior to other nations,—not well founded.   —*Ernest R. Bryan.*

In the choice of a life mate, consider these factors:

Social: Both persons should have a similar background and standard of living, and one to which each has become accustomed.

Respect and admiration: Each should try to realize the other is outstanding.

Physical factors: Health. Physical attractiveness; but other important things should not be overlooked on this account. Physical blemishes apart from ill health do not matter.

Psychological factors: Temperament. Common interests (a few separate interests do no harm, but these should not dominate). Thought and consideration for each other. Mutual confidence and trust. Respect and admiration. Each should have a wholesome attitude toward sex. Sense of humor. Deep mutual affection. Agreement in home planning. Think alike as to children.

Religious and spiritual: Should think alike as to right and wrong. A marriage can be successful even though there are religious differences, but the difficulties are real and sometimes serious.

"No house is large enough for two families." "Engagements should be for a short time only. Use them for planning marriage." —*Rev. Clifford Earle.*

Schedule your leisure. Most inventions were made in leisure time. Many cultural values are possible then. Read in leisure time; especially read the Bible, for it is a beautiful piece of literature as well as our spiritual guide. Visit interesting places in your locality. Enjoy music—but if you fill your mind with jazz, you may find it hard to train yourself to appreciate good music. You have more money when you budget your expenditures; you can budget time with equally good results. —*Dorothy Lehman.*

Better Meetings

The executive committee should meet each month, and plan for one month ahead. The program should be flexible enough to permit desirable changes in plans. The meetings should be advertised effectively.

What interesting and unusual meetings have you attended? Field trips, under best available leadership. Panel discussions. Outdoor meetings, such as vesper service, sunrise service, a meeting under the trees or beside the ocean or a lake, starlight meeting. Questionnaire or check-list type, to discover group interests. Ceremonial type: installation of officers, welcome to new members, home dedication, candlelight ceremony in connection with a special offering. Cottage prayer-meetings. Music and art appreciation.
—*Dr. George Oliver Taylor.*

Have Scripture well read. Have pictures in the room. Provide poems, ritual, drama. Use proper terms in drama: don't say "stage" for "rostrum," don't say "cast" for "characters." Have prayer before the play is presented. Flowers help the worship atmosphere.

To hold your members in the meeting and get all to take part in discussions, give them something to do. Have references to look up, questions to be answered. These are passed out at the door as the young people enter. Don't have many speakers on the program. Leave space for the unplanned participation of members who become interested in the topic.

Why ask the minister to do all the praying? Teach the youth group to pray.
—*Geneva F. Craig.*

Living Devotionally

Ways to make personal devotions helpful: Learn to spend some time each day alone. Learn to think great thoughts when alone. Make prayer an adventure in discovering ways to make the world better. Read the Bible regularly, as well as books about the Bible. Begin the day with "I am going to do my best to cooperate with God." End it with "Father, into Thy hands I commit my spirit." —*Rev. Herbert L. Minard.*

Christian Missions Today

Mr. and Mrs. Abbey sailed in 1929 to India, to assume the general secretaryship of Christian Endeavor there. The post had been vacant ten years and the work had suffered. The Abbeys were traveling in the field for two and a half years, visiting societies and getting acquainted. The India Union's constitution was changed, dividing the country into provinces corresponding to our states, and providing that each provincial union would elect to the India Union board one member and one alternate. The board consists of thirty-six members and alternates who meet every other year; they are in full charge of the work in India.

The Abbeys found a definite need for new literature. The first book prepared dealt with methods; it was printed in English and later in the vernaculars. A monthly magazine, in English, is published and goes throughout India.

Many Christian Endeavor societies have taken the place of churches in situations where the loss of support makes a church impossible. There is a cooperative plan with the India Sunday School Union, so that Christian Endeavor and this union use the same literature and work through and with each other. They are aided by the National Christian Council in coordinating the work.   —*Mrs. Vere W. Abbey.*

Getting the Most from the Bible

These are profitable ways of personal use: Reading a passage at some regular time each day. Following a schedule of reading, in accordance with a denominational or other program (Sunday school lessons, devotional booklets, etc.). Reading until a message strikes home to the individual life. Repeated reading of a single book. Reading biographical passages. Reading a selected class of material (the parables, promises, miracles, etc.). Following a great teaching through the various books (love, faith, hope, etc.).

For more thorough study of the Bible: Reading longer books at one sitting. Coordinated reading of books together, having similar themes or dealing with the same period (Galatians and Romans, Judges and Ruth). Reading with explanatory notes and commentaries. Reading with several translations at hand.

If you memorize, use the King James Version because of its unrivaled beauty of expression. Memorize passages which express your own soul's faith and aspirations. Memorize passages which have time-honored value (like the Twenty-third Psalm, I Corinthians 13). Use regular leisure moments for memorizing (going to and from work).   —*Dr. Frederick W. Cropp.*

New York State Endeavorers supplied volume and color to the Convention parade on Atlantic City's Boardwalk

XII

A Chapter of Greetings

AUSTRALIA

Best wishes! What a mad, inexplicable world we are living in! The one bright spot is that out of the horrors of war will come a closer collaboration and understanding between the great United States of America and the great British Empire.

We often live over again the last World's Convention [held at Melbourne, Australia].

F. H. RALPH, Treasurer,
The National Christian Endeavor Union of Australia.

BOLIVIA

How much it must mean to Endeavorers in the war zones to know that their brothers and sisters in the two Americas are praying for them, and are one with them in heart! How good it is to look forward to the time when war will be forever banished from this earth and the Prince of Peace will reign here in love and justice!

A new Young People's society was formed in this city a few months ago. Similar groups are meeting in others parts of this country, which are one in heart and purpose with Christian Endeavor societies in all parts of the world. May we all, older and younger Endeavorers, be faithful in praying for one another and in laboring for Christ and the church wherever the Lord has placed us.

ANNA WOLFENSBERGER, Cochabama.

CEYLON

As a small boy I came under the influence of the Christian Endeavor union in my village, where my own father, a man in business, was its president. I am always thankful to God for what Christian Endeavor has meant to me personally. Now in turn I am anxious to bring all our young people under its influence.

Since we met in Australia three years ago, God has been pleased to call me to the highest office in our Methodist Church, and I am now chairman of the North Ceylon District of the Methodist Church. It is a position of very great trust and responsibility, and it is the first time in our history that a native of Ceylon has been appointed to this office. I ask you to remember me in your prayers, that God will use and guide me in this noble service.

REV. JAMES S. MATHER, Jaffna.

COLOMBIA

We rejoice with fellow Endeavorers everywhere in the vibrant comradeship made possible through Him who has brought us into true oneness by His redeeming love. With all who are suffering from the devastations of the heinous conflict now raging, we are suffering in minds and souls, and are instant in prayer for a just and lasting peace that would result in true world brotherhood.

Trusting in the Lord Jesus Christ for strength, we are persuaded that nothing will separate us from the love of God. May His grace, mercy, and peace be with you all.

NOEL J. L. GONSALVES, San Andres Island.

GREAT BRITAIN

Please convey my sincere greetings and those of all British Christian Endeavorers to our fellow-workers and members at the Atlantic City Convention.

Despite the disasters consequent upon enemy action, whereby our premises have completely gone, and despite restricted finances, there is a genuine spirit of hopefulness when facing the future. Many societies are regularly meeting, and even in these admittedly critical times, new societies are being formed.

London, Southampton, Portsmouth, Sheffield, Birmingham, Liverpool, Coventry, Plymouth, Belfast are deeply scarred by reason of severe raids, but I have met Endeavorers or heard from them representing all these centers, and they are determined to go forward bravely.

Quite a few of our members have lost their lives, others their homes, many their churches. But Christian Endeavor is still alive to possibilities. I wish I could have spoken in person to your Endeavorers. I could have told them a story that they would never forget, but all over the world the movement will rise again!

ERNEST R. SQUIRE, London.

EUROPEAN UNION

(Cablegram of July 7)

Heartiest greetings from European Union to International Convention. Christian Endeavor still lives in Europe, persecuted but not forsaken, cast down but not destroyed. Troubled as the present is and the future may seem, God is on His throne. He has not lost control. His Kingdom is an everlasting Kingdom, and when in His own providence the dictators are defeated, we will begin again to rebuild the walls of European Christian Endeavor. Warmest greetings to colleagues and love to Mother Clark.

REV. JAMES KELLY, *President*,
European Christian Endeavor Union.

Carroll M. Wright — Homer Rodeheaver

From the Sixtieth Anniversary Radio Message to British Christian Endeavorers

from Christian Endeavorers of North America

By Daniel A. Poling

Fifteen thousand Christian Endeavorers of North America, young people from every province of Canada and every state of the American Union, are now assembled in their Sixtieth Anniversary Convention in Atlantic City, New Jersey. As their President and bearing their commission, I speak their love to and their faith in Christian Endeavorers of the United Kingdom, and indeed all Christian Endeavorers everywhere. Nor should this message be confined to Christian Endeavor. Our fellowship is broader than the bounds of any organization, world-wide though that organization may be. It reaches to young people and friends of young people everywhere.

We are profoundly grateful that in this high hour John Winant is the American Ambassador in London. It is my conviction that he represents, as no other man who might have been chosen, the soul of America. When he speaks, he speaks for us all. Personally, I have known him in practically every circumstance of public life through a generation. Surely God was fitting him for so great a mission, preparing him for this opportunity at once so grave and so sublime.

A few months ago I received a letter from a young English doctor, who, even as I speak to you, moves through London on his errands of healing and mercy. At the heart of his letter is one of the finest sentences that have come out of this war: "We haven't time to hate. It takes all our time to keep ourselves fit to live and perhaps die for something more glorious than life." That young doctor is not a conscientious objector.

Those who now offer their lives, suffer, and die that freedom shall not die, that democracy and the hard-won institutions of liberty shall not perish, offer their lives, suffer, and die for all men, whatever their flags, suffer and die for foes and friends alike. Freedom cannot be isolated, and democracy must at last be for all if it is to be preserved for any.

As we enter upon this task, we have been lifted and challenged by the living faith, the demonstrated loyalty, of our British associates. Your headquarters under London skies is a mass of rubble. Your physical properties have all been destroyed. But in not one element have you ceased to function, and not from a single leader has come the voice of despair.

Again and again we have been shamed by your living faith, by your demonstrated loyalty and courage. To this loyalty and courage, to this faith, we answer now that our Convention has many voices, but one voice has been missing—the voice of defeat. We have faced many problems—and thank God for them all! We have accepted a multitude of tasks. And "trusting in the Lord Jesus Christ for strength," we have made of our Sixtieth Anniversary an open door and shall enter now to possess our heritage of peace and power. We have discovered that there is no room for weaklings and that this is not an hour of compromise. For Christ and for the Church we stir ourselves from the failures we confess, from the delays that shame us, and standing at the "Ready" we lift the united voice, "Speak, Lord, for Thy servant heareth."

Others have called for a new world order. Christian youth now calls for a new world order: a new world order that shall begin in our own hearts, a new world order in which intolerance—intolerance of color, faith or race—shall be the greatest social sin. If Britain and America would be strong, if their defenses—physical, moral and spiritual—are to be adequate, then we must be "brothers all." Without prejudice to our individual loyalties and, indeed, strengthening every worthy loyalty, we must be "brothers all." Black and white, Protestant, Catholic and Jew, now and forever, we must be "brothers all."

XIII

Be It Resolved--

A Response to the President of the United States

Whereas, the Thirty-eighth International Christian Endeavor Convention, meeting in Atlantic City on the sixtieth anniversary of the Christian Endeavor movement, has been profoundly moved by the message of President Roosevelt; and

Whereas, he spoke at a moment in history, clouded by the unpredictable, and as he carried burdens of administration in national affairs perhaps never exceeded by those carried by any of his predecessors;

It is hereby *Resolved* that this sixtieth anniversary Convention express to our President its gratitude for his greeting. Its high note of idealism and faith will be carried back to thousands of American homes, not only as a treasured memory, but as an abiding, inspiring reality.

We assure President Roosevelt of our constant prayers that divine wisdom and guidance will be granted him as he leads America in this time of unparalleled crisis. We pledge to our country and to him, our President, unfaltering loyalty, that the brave hopes of American democracy, with faith in God, shall not perish from the earth.

On the Sixtieth Anniversary of Christian Endeavor

The Thirty-eighth International Christian Endeavor Convention, meeting in Atlantic City, July 8-13, 1941, on the occasion of the sixtieth anniversary of its foundation, desires to place in the record of its proceedings its thankfulness to Almighty God for the blessings of these long and wonderful years.

We believe the movement came from the mind and spirit of God to fill a need in the life of the church in its service to youth. We rejoice that it has girdled the world in a ministry of helpful and fruitful spiritual achievement, training 11,000,000 young people in Christian activity.

More than we can express by words we are thankful that the inspired objective and purpose of the organization still remains unchanged "For Christ and the Church." The changing currents of the years have necessitated no change here. "Always—for Christ and the Church." It is as vivid and imperative for youth in 1941 as in 1881. We reaffirm our fealty and loyalty to that two-fold objective.

We recall with pride and thankfulness that in sixty years only two God-guided leaders have occupied the position of President: Francis E. Clark and Daniel A. Poling. The saintly memory of Dr. Clark is a precious and treasured heritage growing ever richer with the passing years, while the living presence of Mrs. Clark is a perpetual benediction. The radiant leadership of Dr. Poling has given him for all time a place in our affections as he meets every emergency with resilient courage.

We believe that the real needs for a full, purposeful life for youth can still best be served as they come to know the living Christ and following His way associate themselves with others in the corporate life of His Church.

With a song of praise for the past and a shout of faith in the future we renew in prayerful consecration our loyalty to Christian Endeavor.

Greetings to All Endeavorers Everywhere

The Christian Endeavorers of the United States and Canada, gathered in Atlantic City to celebrate the Sixtieth Anniversary of their beloved movement, send their Christian greetings to fellow Endeavorers in every land in all the world.

Our hearts have been saddened and filled with anguish as we have come to know of the sufferings, bereavements and losses of Endeavorers in so many countries. We feel we can only dimly understand the tragedies that envelop their lives. Yet, out of the darkened clouds come stories of glorious devotion to Christ when loyalty to Him often means tribulation and persecution.

With them, we believe that from these testing experiences will come a reborn, purified, and stronger Christian Church, the foundation of which will be their faith in God and His Son, our Saviour.

We would like them to know that they are continually in our prayers, to the end that our Heavenly Father will sustain them by His constant presence. We are conscious of our fellowship with them in Jesus Christ and feel in our common love for Him an unbreakable fellowship. That unity in Christ is unbelievably precious. It is a golden strand that stretches across all barriers on sea and land, race and language, and produces a world-wide international Christian witness.

The Christian faith is an abiding hold on the certainty that there is a light shining in today's darkness proclaiming a God who loves and cares and whose sovereignty is through all time.

Some lights here and there may be blown out by gales of hate and oppression, but ever we hear these words:

"But shall not He who sent him from the door
Relight the lamp once more and yet once more."

May confidence in the final victory of God buttress and sustain the hearts of Christian Endeavorers in all lands and carry them through into the future when "all we have hoped or willed or dreamed of good shall exist." "All nations will be shaken, but," the old prophet continues, "the desire of all nations shall come and I will fill this house with glory, saith the Lord of Hosts." (Haggai 2:7.)

For "God's Order"

Whereas, Dr. Poling in his Presidential Message drew attention to the critical moment in world affairs and challenged us with a constructive program for durable and lasting peace;

Be it hereby *Resolved* that we approve and heartily endorse his seven-point program and commend it to the study, discussion, and action of every society and union.

We especially commend that principle he enunciated for American support of a world agency for the administration of world affairs. Without government there would be anarchy and disorder. Government brings order into city, state, and national life. World relationship is a jurisdiction in which there is no government; and hence there is anarchy. If there is to be justice and ordered happiness in the world, nations must come under the reign of law, as individuals and states give up some of their sovereign prerogatives in the interests of the whole republic. We must think and work and plan for some extension of the concept of federalism.

We cannot do less than hosts of Christian men and women in war-torn lands. They are now striving to lay the foundation not of a European or Oriental order, but of "God's Order."

There is a widespread conviction rising in the churches of Europe that the foundation of a better world must be laid upon the stable foundation of Christian faith if it is to be lasting. The price now being paid in life and treasure demands a world that is saner and more just.

Some day the war will end. God grant that when the long, hard furrow is ploughed we shall be neither too tired, too unprepared, nor too bitter for the tasks of reconciliation and reconstruction.

Our Convention meets to the sound of kingdoms crashing in the night, to the echoing boom of gun and bomb, to the tramp of millions of men in armed strife, to the tortured cries of women and children in beleaguered cities, to the beating wings of the Angel of Death flying over a dozen frontiers, to the wail of starving peoples, to the swift-growing movement of our own land preparing for defense; and yet, even now, as Christians who believe that the final and ultimate truth is the Fatherhood of God and the Brotherhood of Man, we pledge our minds and hearts in helping our beloved country make a contribution to an ordered world life.

Resolution of Thanks

The Thirty-eighth International Convention, meeting on the occasion of its Sixtieth Anniversary, desires to place on permanent record as part of its official proceedings its grateful recognition to all those who have contributed to an historic occasion. This Rainbow Jubilee was an event of the utmost significance in the story of our movement. And with gracious enthusiasm many friends in this city and all over the land have cooperated to make this celebration worthy of the event. Atlantic City 1911 made social, moral, and religious history in America and we feel confident that in the coming years Atlantic City 1941 will be looked upon as a gathering made notable because a vast host of Christian youth found their hearts strangely warmed, thrilled to the blessings and achievements of the past, and in the spirit of high dedication moved into the future.

The Convention desires to thank those who by their efforts helped to make its sessions memorable:

Mr. A. C. Poffenberger and the Convention Committee for untiring and thoughtful efficiency. They were delightful hosts in a fair and famous city.

Mayor Taggart for his official welcome, his key to our President, and particularly for the unusual permission which enabled the parade to be marshalled on the Boardwalk, giving it nationwide publicity.

The chief of police and his staff for courteous and kindly consideration.

Mr. A. J. Morgan of the Convention Bureau, together with Mr. Al Skean and those associated with him in that organization.

Mr. Ed Dougherty, Mr. Dick Morgan, Mr. Eli Briggs, and the auditorium staff for a constant willingness to perfect the machinery of smooth convention operation.

The officials of the Atlantic City Chamber of Commerce and the Atlantic City Council of Boy Scouts.

The ministers and churches of Atlantic City, whose services were especially valuable in the arrangements for the orderly, worshipful, and impressive communion service.

The ushers, whose continuous help evoked our constant praise.

Dr. J. Gordon Howard and the Program Committee for a splendid agenda, the product of months of careful planning, and the denominational youth leaders and our own Field Secretaries and others without whom that planning could not have been carried into such results.

The speakers, whose utterances have lifted all again and again to the very heights of Christian purpose.

Mr. Homer Rodeheaver and his trombone, the organist, the pianist, the soloists and the volunteer choir for adding so greatly to the beauty and spiritual power of every session.

Mrs. Catherine Miller Balm for the conception of a wonderful pageant and rare skill in its presentation.

The newspapers of Atlantic City, the Associated Press, and the papers of the country for their exceptional and generous treatment of Convention news.

The National Broadcasting Corporation and Dr. Walter W. Van Kirk in carrying the spirit and meaning of our gathering by radio all over the land.

The leaders of local, county, and state Unions of the Middle Atlantic Region, whose loyalty and cooperation were invaluable.

Two men particularly, who carried burdens of administration, perhaps beyond the others, yet never lost amid their responsibilities that friendly, kindly touch which has endeared them to Christian Endeavor—Mr. Carroll M. Wright and Dr. Stanley B. Vandersall.

To all who have in any way enabled this mighty throng of young people to enjoy an unforgettable week, in a Christian way, in a lovely city, we extend our thanks.

We say goodby to Atlantic City tonight, but surely life will never be quite the same. We have seen visions, dreamed dreams, drawn blueprints, opened our souls to the life and light of Christ, made great decisions, and now we go home to translate into action the high moments of Atlantic City 1941.

In the past it has been "For Christ and the Church." From now on it will be *"Always—For Christ and the Church."*

For China Relief

Whereas, this Convention has been deeply moved by the presentation of the tremendous and immediate needs of the people of China in their hour of emergency,

Be it hereby *Resolved* that we endorse and commend the Committee for United China Relief, bringing as it does all churches together for this great human cause.

The Widening Movement to "Save the Children"

Whereas, the needs of underprivileged and distressed children, both in America and amid the conditions of war overseas, merit the wholehearted support of World Christian Endeavor,

Be it *Resolved* that we wholeheartedly commend the constructive endeavor of the Save the Children Federation at home and abroad for its present work and as it prepares through the *International Save the Children Union* for the hour of world rebuilding.

Cooperation in Ecumenical Christianity

This Convention rejoices with the Christian youth of the world in the development of the ecumenical movement among the Protestant churches.

Two years ago, the Thirty-seventh International Convention sent its greetings to the World Christian Youth Conference in Amsterdam, Holland. This conference, attended by 1,500 delegates from over seventy nations and countries, was a most significant and successful event. It greatly advanced the ecumenical movement among the youth of the church.

Christian Endeavor is ecumenical in character, and the study of the findings of the Amsterdam Conference is highly recommended.

Christian Endeavor gladly accepts its responsibility. It will joyfully cooperate with all other youth agencies with similar ideals with the hope that Christian youth cooperatively can make a profound impact upon the world in the name of Christ.

On America's Alcohol Problem

The Christian Endeavor movement at its Convention held at Atlantic City in 1911 gave the nation the slogan, "A Saloonless Nation by 1920."

Through the unceasing efforts of Christian men and women across the country national prohibition was achieved in 1920.

As Endeavorers again meet in Atlantic City, it is to find the traffic in beverage alcohol has been revived as a major menace to public morals and civic goodness.

Believing that the liquor traffic must be restricted and prohibited if the people of this country are to live together in sobriety and happiness, we, the delegates at the Atlantic City Convention, 1941,

1. Urge the passage of legislation now pending before Congress restricting the sale of alcoholic beverages in or near Army, Naval, and Air camps, stations, and cantonments;

2. Propose the utmost activity on the part of Christian Endeavorers everywhere leading toward local option, toward the immediate sharp restriction and eventual elimination of liquor advertising, and toward the rigid control of liquor sales;

3. Encourage in our societies, local churches, and public schools, education concerning the nature of alcohol and the individual and social effects of drinking;

4. Heartily commend Allied Youth as our instrument of alcohol education throughout the nation.

Massachusetts Carried American and
Christian Flags

XIV

Special Luncheons and Dinners

Pastors' Luncheon

A large number of local and visiting clergymen attended the Pastors' Luncheon at the Glaslyn Chatham Hotel on July 9. Dr. W. A. MacTaggart of Toronto, Canada, presided with his usual graciousness. Speakers were Rev. Clifford Earle of Chicago and Harry N. Holmes of New York, Vice-President of the International Society of Christian Endeavor.

Mr. Holmes mentioned lack of a world government as the reason for anarchy in the world conditions of today.

"Without government, no matter where it is, you have anarchy," he said. "Our cities and nations, of course, have government. The one area in the world where there is no governmental authority is in the relationship between nations; hence anarchy has come to our international relations.

"The supreme task is to bring world government, so that in place of chaos and danger we shall have order and peace. Something more than a League of Nations is required. There must be world union to enforce international laws."

Missionary Dinner

Mrs. Helen Lyon Jones, whose world travels and abiding concern for the missionary enterprise have made her exceptionally well informed about missions, presided at the Missionary Dinner, held at McIntyre's Restaurant on July 9.

The speakers were Rev. Vere W. Abbey and Mrs. Abbey, of India, and Rev. Philip Lee of China.

Long-Timers' Luncheon

William S. Wise of Pittsburgh presided at a luncheon of more than two hundred "Long-timers" at the Madison Hotel on July 10. Greetings were given by Dr. A. E. Cory, Hon. Frederick A. Wallis, Dr. W. A. MacTaggart, and Clara Dohme.

Dr. Poling and Mr. Wise proposed that the "Long-timers" should form an organization to be known as the Celts (Christian Endeavor Long-timers), which will meet regularly at every International Convention and World's Convention of Christian Endeavor. The idea was received with enthusiasm, and fifty-three of the persons in attendance underwrote some $3,000, as the first step in a comprehensive program to help strengthen the finances of Christian Endeavor in its Rainbow

Jubilee year. Besides, they proposed to take the lead in coming months in planning for many Sixtieth Anniversary Birthday Parties for the benefit of world-wide Christian Endeavor.

The High School Division Banquet is described in a chapter titled "The Diary of John Doe, Jr."

The Official Convention Banquet is briefly reviewed in the same chapter.

Christian Vocations Luncheon

Life Work Recruits and other young people interested in full-time Christian service met at McIntyre's on July 11 for luncheon.

Dr. J. Gordon Howard, chairman of the Convention Program Committee, presided. Those who spoke on the joys and responsibilities of full-time Christian service, mentioning the qualifications of the Life Work Recruit, included Rev. Vere W. Abbey, Dr. Frederick W. Cropp, Rev. Daniel K. Poling, and Genevieve McCulloch.

The two V's — Veh and Vandersall

XV

Preparations for Greater Service

for Christian Endeavor

PROGRAM

MONTHS before the Convention assembled in Atlantic City, there had begun the process of study, discussion, and consultation by which a two-year program of the North American societies and unions is created.

The first work was done in the Educational Council, which is composed of representatives of the International Society's administrative and editorial staff, leaders chosen by the Field Secretaries of Christian Endeavor, and young people's specialists selected by the leaders of young people's work in the Protestant denominations. The Council's plans were undertaken in cooperation with the Topics Committee of the International Society of Christian Endeavor, whose preliminary work on the 1942 topics for Juniors, High School Endeavorers, and Young People also required a clear understanding of the needs and interests of Christian youth.

Headed for the Hotel. The Abbeys at Right

Aided by Dr. Poling, the Atlantic City Convention Program Committee, and many other outstanding friends and leaders of young people, the Educational Council by late spring was in a position to present to the Board of Trustees of the International Society a substantially completed but still tentative program. This proposed many activities and objectives for societies within the framework of five areas or divisions of the young Christian's life and responsibilities.

The consultation with the trustees was fruitful, as always, and when the viewpoints and suggestions of this governing board had been incorporated in the five-point Reconsecration Program, the appealing theme, "Always—For Christ and the Church," was seen to be well exemplified in both the spirit and the substance of these suggestions for the Christian Endeavorer's personal and group action.

The conference plan of the Convention took into consideration the needs and the emphases of the newly approved program. Conference leaders received information about these objectives in time to frame their plans with "Always—For Christ and the Church" emphases in mind. The daily faculty breakfast, counseled by Dr. J. Gordon Howard and planned for all leaders of the conferences and also officers and speakers, was similarly geared to the same plans, which now became a definite roadmap for the advances of the coming two years.

Prominent in the wealth of printed helps offered to Convention-goers was the new Program Guide of Christian Endeavor, presenting in thousands of words the ideas, suggestions, and counsel to make each phase of the program practical and workable in the societies and unions of Christian Endeavor.

The Convention launched the program—like a great new ship, long in the building—and chose a crew to man and command the two years of progress and increased responsibility which these far-visioned and complete plans helped to make ready. As Chapter XI, reviewing many conferences, has revealed, the spirit of the workers' study and discussion at Atlantic City was to exchange and utilize all the ideas that these large and earnest groups of young Endeavorers could marshal. Guided by an experienced leader and chairman, each conference was a school in program-making and in planning voluntary action designed to bring about the advancement of the cause of Christ.

When the last rich hour of the Convention came and departed, the new program had become a living and energized force in Christian youth work "For Christ and the Church." What had once been tentative sentences penciled by earnest leaders in a planning conference had been so thoroughly merged with the thought and action of thousands of alert and willing young Christians that now the 1941-1943 program is a definite product and reminder of Atlantic City 1941—as of course was intended and desired. The pages of this Report help to give color and depth to the program of Christian youth's rededication—"Always—For Christ and the Church."

The program is printed in full in the concluding pages of this book.

ORGANIZATION

On July 8, 1941, the Board of Trustees of the International Society took action that had been proposed by Dr. Poling and other leaders who have become keenly aware of the world situation and of Christian Endeavor's overwhelming challenges and responsibilities growing out of that situation.

The following day the International Society's recommendations dealing with the emergency organization needs were presented to the Executive Committee of the World's Christian Endeavor Union, which discussed all details of the proposal and accepted the plan in full.

By reason of their intrinsic importance, these details of the official action taken to meet an emergency in world affairs and in Christian work deserve a place in this Report of the Rainbow Jubilee Convention. Beyond that, there seems to many of us to be deep historic importance in the forthright action of the leaders and counselors of the Christian Endeavor movement to secure the maximum of service possibilities with a minimum of expenditure, lost motion, and delay in meeting the imminent responsibilities.

The following paragraphs are taken from the minutes of the Executive Committee of the World's Union:

A Recommendation from the International Society of Christian Endeavor

1. That the trustees of the International Society of Christian Endeavor recognize the existence of a period of world emergency, calling for the conservation of men, money, and activities, so that the best results may be obtained with the least overhead expense and with the least possible duplication of personnel and program; that the activities of the International Society of Christian Endeavor and of the World's Christian Endeavor Union be carried on by the World's Christian Endeavor Union during the period of world emergency; and that this action be operative until the Executive Committee and the trustees of the World's Christian Endeavor Union shall declare the emergency ended.

(a) This action shall not affect the life and corporate existence of the International Society of Christian Endeavor, all legal requirements for officers, meetings, etc., being met.

2. That the trustees of the International Society of Christian Endeavor request the Executive Committee of the World's Christian Endeavor Union to accept temporary responsibility for carrying on the program of the International Society of Christian Endeavor; that we further request the World's Christian Endeavor Union to make grants to the International Society of Christian Endeavor as it is able, these grants to assist the International Society of Christian Endeavor in meeting financial obligations, including current debts, obligations for the headquarters building, obligations to annuitants, etc. In this connection, we ask the President and his Boston associates, in meeting the world emergency, to reduce to a final minimum all headquarters expense in Boston.

3. That the trustees of the International Society of Christian Endeavor request the World's Christian Endeavor Union to assume responsibility for making all financial

appeals, including the appeals in this Convention, for Christian Endeavor at home and abroad, and covering as much of the work heretofore done by both organizations as may be determined. We specifically request that in this Convention the Sixtieth Anniversary Rehabilitation or Restoration Fund be presented with utmost fidelity; that the remainder of our anniversary year be used to the utmost to secure a possible $60,000 in addition to current income, this special fund to include possible grants to the International Society to apply on its indebtedness and to provide for the future of Christian Endeavor at home and abroad.

4. That, since the by-laws of the World's Christian Endeavor Union provide for annual memberships, the trustees of the International Society of Christian Endeavor request the annual members in the International Society, beginning in 1942, to transfer their memberships to the World's Christian Endeavor Union, the membership dues being payable to the World's Christian Endeavor Union.

In general outline, we believe these recommendations to meet the imperative requirements of the present world emergency. They represent the unanimous conclusion not only of your President and of his executive associates in Boston, but of your trustees. They would concentrate responsibility and leadership in one organization. Actually the adjustment is simple, because personnel is almost identical. These recommendations if accepted would, we believe, make it possible for us to hold and extend the lines at home to overcome any spirit of defeatism, to serve states, unions, and societies from headquarters as we have not been able to serve, and to achieve cohesive power.

The adoption of these recommendations would enable your President and his associates and your Executive Committee with enthusiasm to give the maximum of their efforts not only to solve the problems of the past, but to meet successfully the requirements of the present world emergency and world opportunity.

All channels of cooperation between Christian Endeavor and the other organizations in the young people's field continue as heretofore, coming now under the authorization and responsibilities of the Executive Committee of the World's Union.

The Union of Field Secretaries and Denominational Young People's Workers continues to operate as formerly, and will engage in work as a creative body in behalf of Christian Endeavor.

Recommendations on materials and educational policy from these and other sources come to the Educational Council of the International Society through the World's Union Executive Committee.

The Topics Committee, *Christian Endeavor World*, and departments and regions of the International Society have a close and cohesive relationship to the World's Union, its officers, and the world-wide span of its work and duties.

Thus strengthened and invigorated, the organization machinery of North American Christian Endeavor becomes a more definite and useful world service agency for the cause of Christ.

LEADERSHIP

The officers chosen for new terms, beginning at Atlantic City and carrying into the months of the new advance and enhanced obligations announced in these pages, are named in the following pages.

INTERNATIONAL SOCIETY OF CHRISTIAN ENDEAVOR

President	Dr. Daniel A. Poling
Associate President	Miss Pauline Shoemaker
Honorary Vice-president	Dr. William Hiram Foulkes
Vice-president	Harry N. Holmes
Vice-president	Mrs. Helen Lyon Jones
Vice-president	Dr. J. Gordon Howard
Vice-president	Dr. Norman Vincent Peale
Vice-president	Rev. Lawrence W. Bash
Executive Secretary, Treasurer, and Superintendent of Travel	Carroll M. Wright
Associate and Recording Secretary, Superintendent of Christian Vocations, Acting Treasurer, Clerk ISCE Corporation	Dr. Stanley B. Vandersall
Field Secretary	Ernest S. Marks
Auditor	William J. von Minden

Vice-presidents in Charge of Regions

North Atlantic (Maine, N.H., V·, Mass., R.I., Conn., N.Y.)	Eugene G. Alhart
Middle Atlantic (Pa., N.J., Del., D.C., Md., W.Va.)	Arch J. McQuilkin
Southern (Va., N.C., S.C., Fla., Ga., Ala., Miss., Tenn., Ky.)	James A. Huff, Jr.
Great Lakes (Ohio, Ind., Ill., Mich., Wis.)	Rev. Harvey C. Hahn
Central (Iowa, Minn., Neb., Kans., Mo., N.D., S.D.)	Assigned to Rev. Lawrence W. Bash
Pacific (Wash., Ore., Calif., Ida., Utah, Mont., Nev., Hawaii, Alaska)	H. Lewis Mathewson
Rocky Mountain (Wyo., Colo., Ariz., N. Mex.)	Myron M. Orton
Southwestern (Ark., La., Okla., Texas)	J. Stuart Pearce, Jr.
Dominion of Canada	George J. McQueen

Departmental Superintendents

Adult and Alumni	Miss F. Lillian Rodenhi
Christian Citizenship	Miss Nelle Zuyddyk
Devotional (Prayer Meeting)	Mrs. John R. Strome
Extension and Lookout	Ralph G. Gillespie
High School (Intermediate)	Mrs. L. C. Greene
Junior	Miss Sara McCloy
Missionary	Miss Genevieve Bartholomew
Quiet Hour	Miss Wilma C. Loebe
Social and Recreation	Mrs. Catherine Miller Balm
Tenth Legion	Mrs. Reba C. Rickman
World Peace	Ernest R. Bryan

Executive Committee

Albert Arend	H. Lewis Mathewson
Rev. Lawrence W. Bash	Frederick L. Mintel
Bert H. Davis	Dr. Norman Vincent Peale
Dr. William Hiram Foulkes	Dr. Daniel A. Poling
Harry N. Holmes	Miss Pauline Shoemaker
Warren G. Hoopes	Rev. Arthur J. Stanley
Dr. J. Gordon Howard	Dr. Raymond M. Veh
Mrs. Helen Lyon Jones	William J. von Minden
Norman Klauder	Paul M. Williams

WORLD'S CHRISTIAN ENDEAVOR UNION

President .... Dr. Daniel A. Poling
Honorary Vice-president .... Mrs. Francis E. Clark
Vice-president .... Dr. James Kelly (Scotland)
Vice-president .... George H. Nelson (Australia)
Vice-president .... Lionel B. Fletcher (New Zealand)
Honorary Field Secretary .... Harry N. Holmes
General Secretary .... Stanley B. Vandersall
Executive Secretary and Treasurer .... Carroll M. Wright
Auditor .... William J. von Minden

Executive Committee

Rev. Vere W. Abbey
Albert Arend
Rev. Lawrence W. Bash
Dr. A. E. Cory
Bert H. Davis
R. H. Edwin Espy
Dr. William Hiram Foulkes
Harry N. Holmes
Dr. J. Gordon Howard
Warren G. Hoopes
Mrs. Helen Lyon Jones
Dr. Adolph Keller
Harry W. Keller

Norman Klauder
Harry G. Kuch
Ernest S. Marks
H. Lewis Mathewson
Frederick L. Mintel
Dr. Daniel A. Poling
Miss Pauline Shoemaker
Rev. Arthur J. Stanley
Dr. Stanley B. Vandersall
Dr. Raymond M. Veh
William J. von Minden
Paul M. Williams
Carroll M. Wright

CHRISTIAN YOUTH'S REDEDICATION

A Program of Aims and Activities

for

Christian Endeavor Societies and Unions

1941-1943

"ALWAYS --- FOR CHRIST AND THE CHURCH"

Adopted by the Board of Trustees of the International Society of Christian Endeavor and released at the biennial International Convention at Atlantic City, New Jersey, July 8-13, 1941

I. PERSONAL CHRISTIAN EXPERIENCE AND GROWTH.

   A. *Aim to have every active Endeavorer definitely acknowledge his open commitment to Jesus Christ as Saviour and Lord.*

   B. *Deepen the convictions of young people on basic points of Christian belief.*
   Study the doctrinal developments in the church through the centuries, giving special attention to the early church and the Protestant Reformation.

   C. *Encourage young people to speak in testimony of their Christian experience.*

   D. *Use the Christian Endeavor covenant as a basis of membership, relating the individual to Christ, to the society, to the local church, and to the Christian church around the world.*

E. *Challenge every active Endeavorer to strive for personal growth in Christian living.*

Recognize always the supreme authority of Christ in all matters of personal and social conduct.

Make a habit of Bible study.

Establish private devotional practices.

Participate frequently in public worship.

Cultivate Christian friendships.

Seek the spiritual benefits resulting from wide international and inter-racial contacts.

Lay the foundations for happy and successful home life.

Use personal problems and difficulties as definite channels to dependence on God.

F. *Strive for definite growth in the entire Christian Endeavor society.*

Enroll every reachable person as a Comrade of the Quiet Hour.

Promote regular attendance at the worship services of the church.

Enlist Endeavorers and other Christians as tithers, and enroll them as members of the Tenth Legion.

Set every Endeavorer actively at work in the society and church, each having one or more specific tasks and responsibilities.

Encourage all members to influence others to commit their lives to Christ, using such means as

prayer groups,

personal workers' bands,

pre-Easter meetings,

decision services,

pastors' study classes.

Promote participation in active enterprises of the Kingdom, such as the missionary cause, Christian citizenship, secular and religious education, and the like.

G. *Plan the devotional meetings so as to provide maximum opportunities for Christian growth.*

H. *Establish some plan of personal counseling on the problems of young people, such as*

(1) Facing questions relating to personality, religious life, home and marriage, duty to the state;

(2) Choosing vocations in terms of Christian principles, even when first and second preferences are not possible;

(3) Finding Christian values in one's work;

(4) Using recreation as a means of character growth.

II. CHURCH LOYALTY AND FELLOWSHIP.

A. *Improve the members' acquaintance with the history and doctrines of the Christian church, and of their own denomination in particular.*

B. *Encourage young people to be loyal, thorough, and effective in church membership, church attendance, church financial support.*

C. *Share actively in the total educational program of the church.*
Assume an active part in the church-wide program for youth, including the plans, emphases, and activities for young people in the local church and in the denomination.
Promote leadership training classes and courses.
Establish Graded Christian Endeavor (one society, or more, for each definite age group).
Provide for an adult counselor for each High School and Young People's society.
Promote attendance of Endeavorers at denominational youth rallies and summer camps and conferences.
Secure representation of each society in the church's committee on young people's work (or Christian education).

D. *Enrich public and private worship by study and adaptation of the methods and elements of worship.*

E. *Emphasize through study and example the principle that every Christian is a steward of his time, talents, money, and life, all of which belong to God.*

F. *Stress the responsibility of the society in training leaders in church work.*

G. *Dedicate individuals and the group to definite forward steps in helping the church to grow and to serve.*
(Examples: evangelistic campaign sponsored or aided; the work of the Sunday School fostered; united Christian program in the community promoted; responsibilities in citizenship declared and exercised.)

H. *Promote the principles and program of the United Christian Education Advance.*

III. PUTTING CHRISTIANITY INTO ACTION.

A. *Unite with other Christian forces to evangelize the community.*
(Examples: local missions, public meetings, community vacation Bible schools, home visitation, etc.)

B. *Emphasize a practical day-by-day relationship between Christian principles and personal conduct.*

C. *Promote the principle of maintaining those friendships that challenge a young person to his best.*

D. *Inspire young people to make diligent use of school opportunities and to be true to the highest ideals of character.*

E. *Foster Christian principles in home life, such as patience, tact, consideration and understanding between youth and adults, sharing of responsibilities and tasks.*

F. *Aid young people by counseling, study courses, and suitable literature to hold to high standards in the choice of a life partner and preparation for marriage and home life.*

G. *Sponsor and conduct recreational programs that will improve the use of leisure time.*

> Raise the quality of Christian Endeavor recreational events, give them more variety, and open them on occasion to larger numbers of the youth of the community.
>
> Join with other agencies (such as schools and colleges, Christian Associations, Allied Youth, and athletic leagues) in setting higher standards for youth's good times.
>
> Locate specialists in the various constructive hobbies and cultural interests, helping young people to know these men and women and to learn new skills and interests from them.

H. *Educate concerning the harmful effects of alcohol and other narcotics, including tobacco.*

> Campaign against advertising for liquor and cigarettes, in whatever medium used: magazines, outdoor posters, newspapers, moving pictures, radio.
>
> Encourage and assist in organizing Allied Youth Posts in high schools.
>
> Plan education against narcotics, utilizing meetings, addresses, books, charts, laboratory demonstrations, quiz programs, radio presentations, etc.
>
> Support local, and larger, campaigns for strict regulation of the liquor trade, including restriction of hours of sale, looking toward elimination of the sale of alcoholic beverages.
>
> Enlist in campaigns for total abstinence from the use of beverage alcohol and tobacco.

I. *Encourage a wise choice of vocations, and the study of ethical standards applying to the working world.*

J. *Join with other constructive forces for civic betterment.*

> Promote law observance and enforcement.
>
> Remedy prejudice and injustice.
>
> Preserve Sunday, the Lord's Day, from commercialism and irreligious uses.

Deal with the issues of gambling, unwholesome moving pictures, harmful reading matter, habit-forming drugs, the use of beverage alcohol and tobacco, and all other forces detrimental to the Christian development of youth.

Strengthen organizations and programs which aid inter-racial goodwill and the preservation of minority rights.

K. *Support and strengthen Christian Endeavor union work in community, state (province) and nation, as an aid to unity through fellowship and cooperative action.*

IV. MAKING OUR NATION CHRISTIAN.

A. *Support home, or national, missions through educational programs, financial support, and service to the missionary cause.*

Maintain a circulating library of mission books and magazines. Provide study classes, trips to mission centers, and other activities in missionary fact-finding.

Recognize national denominational missions in the society budget. Assist missionary work through donations of clothing, supplies, and toys.

B. *Share in goodwill activities on behalf of minority races and groups, especially in cooperation with other youth agencies, and as presented by the United Christian Youth Movement.*

Know the facts behind prejudices held against minorities. Encourage friendly relations with other races and faiths. Strengthen goodwill among Catholics, Jews, and Protestants.

C. *Join with other agencies and movements to help our nation to be a real haven and home to those who come here from lands of oppression.*

Welcome representative refugees as speakers and social guests in Christian Endeavor gatherings.

Be helpful to groups that acquaint the newcomers with our language and customs and aid them to become self-supporting.

D. *Encourage study and action that will deal with the needs of underprivileged groups.*

Search for lonely and friendless persons and groups, aiding them to find comfort, enlightenment, and comradeship. Promote union programs and activities that strengthen social and economic welfare projects.

Offer aid and support to established religious and secular agencies in the field of social welfare.

E. *Enlist youth for educational and civic campaigns to deal with the problems of liquor, other narcotics, gambling, and unwholesome forms of amusement.*

Acquire and circulate facts about the relation of drinking, smoking, and unworthy amusements to health, public safety, delinquency, and crime.

Encourage wholesome, non-commercial forms of youth recreation that serve as worthy alternatives to forms of relaxation that debase character.

Take an active part in every battle of the continuous campaign against liquor and kindred evils.

F. *Study the causes of crime, and arrive at ideals and practices that seek to offset these causes and to set worthy examples for young people.*

G. *Foster an intelligent love of country and of the Christian principle of democracy.*

Study and discuss the dependence of the democratic principle on those ideals and attitudes that grow out of Christian teachings.

Encourage the practice of democracy in all phases of group life, respecting minority viewpoints and protecting freedom of discussion.

Emphasize the faithful discharge of the responsibilities of citizenship, including the vote, jury duty, protection of public safety, and such participation in national security as conscience permits.

Maintain helpful contacts with Endeavorers and other young people engaged in the service of their country.

Share with Christian youth groups and other worthy youth agencies in efforts to safeguard liberty and justice for all.

V.   MAKING OUR WORLD CHRISTIAN.

A. *Support Christian missions around the world.*

Promote world missions by prayer, educational programs, posters, circulation of mission books and magazines, study classes, drama, films, correspondence, and guest speakers.

Contribute to denominational and interdenominational missionary activities, the latter to include the strategic and influential work of the World's Christian Endeavor Union in mission lands.

B. *Support the cause of peace around the world.*

Seek to make world peace real and practical by striving to achieve its ideals in daily conduct and in local areas.

Promote reading, study, and discussion of the conditions which make for war in the world; likewise study and discuss the basic reasons for peace and ways of attaining lasting peace. Use drama, films, and other means of creating sentiment for peace.

Adopt and promote the Seven-Point Program for Peace as approved by the International Society of Christian Endeavor and other denominational and interdenominational bodies.

Carry out the recommendations of the Peace Department of the International Society in study and action on the subject of peace.

Assist in making the attainment of world peace a major element in the devotional life and in the lifetime ideals of young people everywhere.

C. *Join with other agencies in fostering the preservation of democratic ideals throughout the world.*

D. *Study the causes of economic injustice in the world and the resultant widespread poverty, unrest, and starvation.*

Join with others in efforts to relieve human suffering whereever found.

Seek to overcome attitudes of selfishness, aggression, and lust for power.

Establish and practice personal and group ideals in the use of money, in stewardship, and in relationships toward all mankind.

E. *Work toward a world-wide youth fellowship in which Christian principles may prevail.*

Study the history and culture of other peoples and their contributions to mankind.

Read and discuss articles on youth movements in other countries, especially those based on Christian principles.

Establish means for cooperation in common Christian aims and activities, and participation in correspondence, conferences, conventions, and other methods of bringing together the youth of the world.